WAR, WOMEN,
AND THE NEWS

WAR, WOMEN, AND THE NEWS

How Female Journalists Won the Battle to Cover World War II

Catherine Gourley

ATHENEUM BOOKS FOR YOUNG READERS

NEW YORK LONDON TORONTO SYDNEY

ATHENEUM BOOKS FOR YOUNG READERS
An imprint of Simon & Schuster Children's Publishing Division
1230 Avenue of the Americas
New York, New York 10020

Book design by Valerie Trucchia
The text for this book is set in Miller Daily one.

Manufactured in the United States of America
First Edition
10 9 8 7 6 5 4 3 2 1

LIBRARY OF CONGRESS CATALOGING-IN-PUBLICATION DATA
Gourley, Catherine, 1950–
War, women, and the news: how female journalists won the battle to cover World
War II / Catherine Gourley.—1st ed.
p.   cm.
ISBN-13: 978-0-689-87752-0
ISBN-10: 0-689-87752-8
1. World War, 1939-1945—Journalists—Juvenile literature. 2. Women war corre-
spondents—History—20th century—Juvenile literature. 3. War correspondents—
History—20th century—Juvenile literature. 4. World War, 1939-1945—Press
coverage—Juvenile literature. I. Title.
D798.G68 2007
070'.082'0973—dc22   2005020269

To the next generation of readers: Drew
and Kaylee, Joseph and Katie, and Sydney

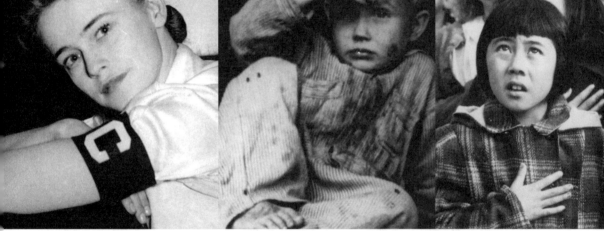

CONTENTS

FOREWORD

A writer's work is like a photograph album or scrapbook, a series of images and memories pasted one page after another. The writer faces two challenges: First, which stories and images should I include? Second, what is the best way to arrange the stories and images so that they tell an interesting and suspenseful story?

In writing *War, Women, and the News*, the selection and sequencing of stories and images was difficult. I found so many published articles and photographs that I liked, but I could not use them all, nor could I run an entire article. I had to select not only which stories to feature but also which passages from those stories.

I have always loved the hunt—uncovering forgotten anecdotes of strong-willed men and women in history. In the three years I spent researching and writing this book, the passion of Martha Gellhorn, the haunting memories of Lee Miller, the unselfish dedication of Dickey Chapelle, and the cocky confidence of Marguerite Higgins were inspiring. And so, as with every photograph album, the stories and photographs within these pages are personal. They reflect just one author's vision and bias.

I hope the readers, both young and old, who take this journey back in time with me to the Second World War will be equally moved by these women who refused to be left behind.

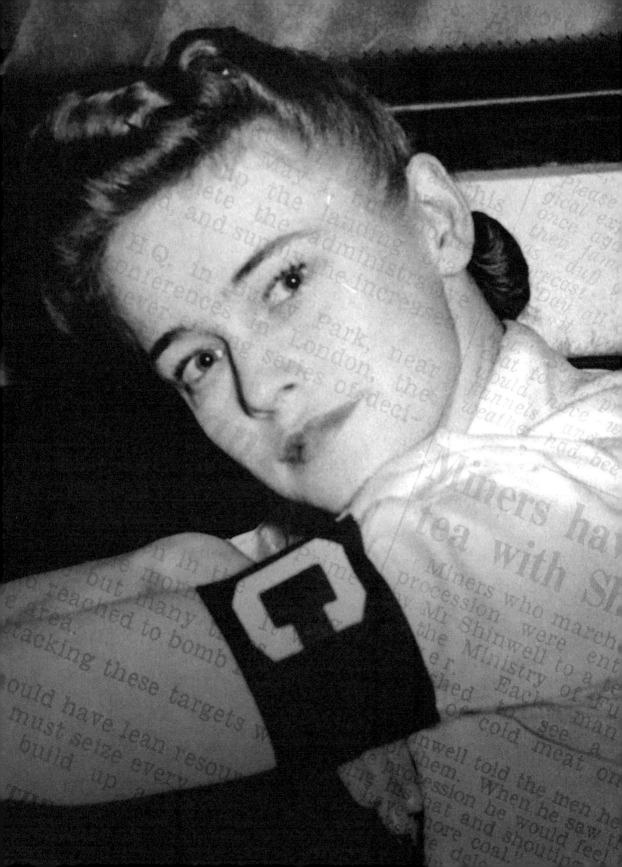

THE WOMEN

On a morning in May 1942, Dickey Chapelle stood in a small office of the War Department in Washington, DC. The day was hot. The room was hotter. Dickey was nervous. More than anything else, she wanted to be a combat photographer. The person who could make that happen was sitting in front of her. On Colonel Dupuy's desk were official papers from the War Department. If the colonel signed those papers, then Dickey Chapelle would be assigned to the Fourteenth Infantry as a war correspondent.

*L*ook magazine had recently published three of her photographs. But Dickey Chapelle was just twenty-three years old. She was not as experienced as other photographers. And she was

In 1942 Dickey Chapelle proudly wore the armband of an accredited news war correspondent.

female. The odds were against her.

Finally, the colonel looked up and asked, "You realize, Mrs. Chapelle, that troops in the field have no facilities for women?"

Dickey stared at him. Was the colonel really asking her about bathrooms? What about her skill as a photographer? Would the War Department actually deny her the opportunity to photograph the war because there wasn't a "ladies' room" on the battlefield?

Dickey blurted out the first thing that came into her mind: "Colonel, I'm sure the Fourteenth Infantry has solved much tougher problems than that, and they'll probably think of a way to lick this one, too." [1]

For a few moments her fate hung in midair. Then the colonel picked up his pen and signed the papers.

Dickey could not have known then how war would forever change her life. Nor could she have imagined how she—one of the few women war correspondents of World War II—would change society's attitudes about women in general. Years later, long after World War II had ended, female writers and photographers would enter the world of journalism through doors Dickey and women like her had opened.

Who were the women who opened these doors? Like Dickey, they had dreams of becoming a writer or a photographer. Getting a job in a mostly all-male newsroom wasn't easy, however, even though most had graduated from college. Marguerite Higgins graduated with honors at the top of her class in 1941. Still, the editor of the *New York Herald Tribune* turned her down. He did not want to hire a woman reporter.

A few of these women had dropped out of college. Bored with textbooks, Martha Gellhorn believed the only way to learn about the world was to travel and meet as many different kinds of people as she could. She discovered she didn't like some of the people she encountered. In Europe she witnessed Nazis bullying Jewish men and women, and she felt disgust. In Spain she saw soldiers dying in the streets. No one asked her to write about the war in that country, but she did anyway. She sent her story to an editor at *Collier's*, a popular magazine back home in the United States. When the magazine published her story and asked for more, her life as a war correspondent began.

The women correspondents read books and newspapers and magazines. They argued—often very passionately—about what they had read and what they had seen. They were curious. They were also skeptical. When Nazi dictator Adolf Hitler signed a peace treaty with Poland and then another with Russia, both Sigrid Schultz and Dorothy Thompson warned their readers that Hitler could not be trusted.

Before the war most of these women had lived for a few years or more in a foreign country. Most could speak French or German or Italian. Some, like Therese Bonney, could speak French, German, *and* Italian. They carried passports that allowed them to cross the border of one country into another.

Once the war began, the borders closed. Military blockades controlled who entered and left countries. Now the correspondents carried different papers—military credentials from the War Department. Only those journalists with credentials could enter combat areas. The War Department assigned credentials to 558 print and radio correspondents. Of these, 127 were women.

They were not soldiers, but they wore military uniforms. Stitched on the upper sleeve of their uniforms was a yellow *C* for "correspondent." Instead of dresses and perfume, their suitcases held cameras and flashbulbs, typewriter ribbons and sheets of carbon paper.

A few, like Dickey Chapelle, were married. But a reporter must go where news is happening. Married women often found that being away for months from their homes and husbands was difficult. For some, their marriages ended before the war did.

They were stubborn. They did not take no for an answer when commanding officers refused to send them to the front lines because they were women. When Ruth Cowan landed in Algiers, Africa, the head of the Associated Press said he did not want any women attached to his unit. The ship was going back to America the next day, and he ordered Ruth to be on it. She refused to leave.

A short time later Ruth Cowan landed an interview with one of the most important generals in the American army, George Patton.

Before the war much of society had believed women were fragile creatures who lacked the mental skills to interpret the news. One newspaper editor described women journalists this way: "When criticized, they sulk and burst into tears. They depend on men to help them in tough spots, then double-cross them." [2]

Even after the war began, many editors and military officers still believed these stereotypes about women. Under fire, they'd cower. The *ack-ack* of machine guns would surely shatter their nerves. When confronted with blood and brutality on the battlefield, they'd cover their eyes and sob. Worse, soldiers would risk their lives and their missions to rescue these women from harm's way.

That's not what happened. They did not need rescuing. At times they cowered and cried, just as soldiers cowered and cried. They sometimes faltered and made mistakes. The first time Dickey Chapelle came under enemy fire, she was aboard a ship in the South Pacific. She was shaking so badly, the camera wobbled in her hands. She didn't take a single photograph of the Japanese bomber that fired upon her ship.

The women wrote about the war for the same reasons that men

correspondents did. Martha Gellhorn wanted to learn the truth. The only way to do that, she said, was to witness the war herself. Photographer Dickey Chapelle believed in the war's mission—to stop totalitarian rule in Europe and in Asia. She said she would never forget (nor did she want to) that she was one of almost one million Americans who shared a single aim—to defeat evil in the world. That mission was more important than whether she lived or died. [3]

Still others went to war because it was the biggest news story of their lives and they did not want to be left out. They were journalists, first and foremost, and as journalists, their responsibility was to get the story. Most women said they had done nothing extraordinary in being a war correspondent. They had simply completed their job the best way they knew how. None bragged that they were brave. The war frightened and at times even horrified them. Still, reporting from the edge of battlefields was also thrilling. After eight weeks on the German front, Marguerite Higgins discovered that "being afraid is seldom boring."

They were loners but not unfriendly. They knew how to strike up a conversation with strangers, asking questions that became the stuff of their stories and photographs. They were often very clever, figuring out ways to hitchhike a ride in a jeep to where a war story was happening.

This book tells the story of their journey. It begins in America in the 1930s during a period called the Great Depression. Many Americans were out of work, hungry, and homeless. Countries around the world also suffered from economic hard times. During the Great Depression many women got their first opportunity to work in journalism. During this Great Depression, too, the first guns of World War II echoed across Europe.

Dundee
Leith to Copenhagen 610
Kristiansand
Skager Rak
Skaw
L. Wetter
Jönköping
F. of Forth
Edinburgh
N O R T H
S E A
Gothenburg
(Göteborg)
Aalborg
Kattegat
Kalmar
Newcastle
Sunderland
Denmark
Jutland
Aarhus
Sound
Hälsingborg
Dogger Bank
London to Oslo 650
Leningrad 1207
Esbjerg
Copenhagen
Malmö
Middlesbrough
York
Fyen
Zealand
Hull
Manchester
Sheffield
Flensburg
Heligoland
Bornholm
Lolland
The Wash
Stralsund
Rügen
Frisian Is.
L. to H. 427
Kiel
Norwich
Texel
Helder
Lübeck
Rostock
Yarmouth
Birmingham
Emden
Groningen
Hamburg
Stettin
Amsterdam
Hague
Holland
Zuider Zee
Bremen
Elbe
LONDON
Harwich 122
Rotterdam
Hanover
Charlottenburg
BERLIN
Thames
Flushing
Arnhem
Brighton
Ostend
Str. of Dover
Brunswick
Magdeburg
Portsmouth
Calais
Ghent
Antwerp
G e r m a n y
Krefeld
Essen
Dortmund
Boulogne
Brussels
Elberfeld
Dieppe
Belgium
Lille
Düsseldorf
Kassel
Halle
Leipzig
Görlitz
Cologne
Aix la Chapelle
Erfurt
Dresden
Amiens
Rouen
Seine
Ardennes
Liége
Wiesbaden
Chemnitz
Ore Mts.
Plauen
Reims
Sedan
Luxemburg
Frankfurt
Mayence
Darmstadt
Prague
Elbe
Versailles
PARIS
Châlons
Metz
Würzburg
Pilsen
Bohemia
Le Mans
Chartres
Marne
Strasbourg
Mannheim
Karlsruhe
Nürnberg
Iglau
Orléans
Troyes
Nancy
Vosges
Stuttgart
Ratisbon
Black Forest
Tours
Cher
Mulhouse
Belfort
Danube
Augsburg
Budweis
Brno
Bourges
Dijon
Freiburg
Munich
Linz
Nevers
Besançon
Basle
(Basel)
L. of Constance
Zürich
Salzburg
VIENNA
le Creuzot
Saône
Châlon
Berne
Switzerland
Innsbruck
Limoges
Loire
Allier
St. Gotthard
Geneva
Clermont
Graz
M. Dore
Simplon
Mt. Blanc 15780
S. Etienne
Lyons
Mt. Cenis
Trento
Laibach
(Ljubljana)
Milan
Brescia
Gorizia
Lot
Grenoble
Padua
Trieste
Tarn
Turin
Po
Mantua
Verona
Venice
Fiume
Rhône
Alessandria
Genoa
Pola
Montpellier
Nîmes
Avignon
Parma
Modena
Monaco
G. of Genoa
Spezia
Ravenna
Nice
Riviera
Bologna
Narbonne
Marseilles
Cannes
Toulon
S. Marino
Dinaric
G. of Lion
(G. of Lions)
Leghorn
Arno
Florence
Sebenico
Ancona
Perpignan
Hyères Is.
C. Corse
Siena
Perugia
Split
Bastia

> " I am giving you this picture as I have been able to see it and through the eyes of the people with whom I talked. Grim is a gentle word: it's heartbreaking and terrifying. "
>
> *MARTHA GELLHORN, NOVEMBER 25, 1934

Chapter One

FEAR ITSELF

On a May morning in 1927, bells rang on Teletype machines in newsrooms across Europe and the United States. In just thirty-three and one half hours Charles Lindbergh had flown nonstop from New York to Paris, France. No one had ever accomplished such an amazing feat! Suddenly, the Atlantic Ocean that separated two continents seemed a little less grand. The world became a little smaller. Before his historic flight few knew who Charles Lindbergh was. But the moment the Spirit of Saint Louis *bounced onto the landing field in France and the young aviator stepped from the cockpit, "Lucky Lindy" became big news. He was a hero.*

Nine months earlier a nineteen-year-old woman named Gertrude Ederle had also earned the admiration of the world. She did not fly on wings across an ocean. Rather, with the power of only her strong legs and lungs, she swam across the icy English Channel. For fourteen hours and thirty-one minutes she swam. Rain fell. Strong currents sucked at her kicking legs, trying to pull her back to the coast of France. Waves rose up and slapped her face and stole her breath. At last she spied the cliffs of Dover on the English coastline. On shore a crowd of people, reporters among them, cheered for her. Some splashed into the surf to help her out of the water.

Trudy, too, had become a hero.

In the 1920s, people wanted to believe in heroes. The world was still reeling from the wounds of a terrible world war. Hundreds of thousands of soldiers had died in Europe. Those who had survived returned to their homes haunted by what they had experienced on the battlefield. The Great War, as people called World War I then, had been so brutal and bloody that leaders of countries swore another world war could never happen again.

They were wrong.

The Great War changed America. Young people, in particular, were rebellious. Young women changed how they dressed. Gone were the tight-fitting corsets and long sweeping skirts their mothers had worn. They bobbed their hair shockingly short and wore thin, shapeless dresses that revealed—for the first time ever—their knees. Gone, too, were the old social traditions that said a woman's place was in the home taking care of her husband

Photographs like this helped the United States government better understand the hardship Americans were experiencing during the Great Depression in the 1930s.

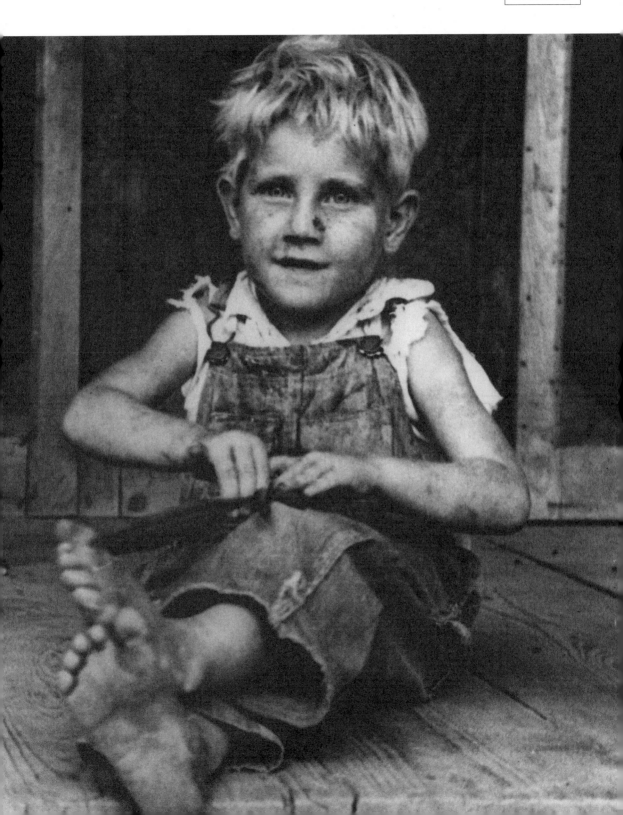

and children. More young women went to college than ever before. They took jobs as secretaries and typists, teachers and nurses. They joined the staffs of newspapers and magazines.

The automobile gave young people new freedoms their parents never had. Men and women drove about together, unchaperoned. Instead of waltzing to the music of an orchestra, they danced the Charleston—wildly kicking their legs and swinging their arms. Congress had outlawed alcohol, but gangsters still made and sold "bootleg," or illegal, liquor. Men and women, both young and old, knocked on the doors of "speakeasies," private clubs where they could buy the bootleg alcohol. The decade was so rowdy that this period of American history became known as the Roaring Twenties. It was as if America wanted to forget the old ways that had brought so much death and destruction to the world.

In the 1920s, the country was "in a mood for magic," wrote journalist Anne O'Hare McCormick. Magic was the belief that anyone could accomplish their dreams, as Lucky Lindy and Trudy Ederle had. Magic was also the belief that anyone in America could one day become rich or famous. Andrew Carnegie had done it. As a boy, he had worked in a cotton factory in Pittsburgh. By the time of his death he had become one of the wealthiest men in the world. Henry Ford had tinkered with clocks and watches in the farmhouse where he was born. By the 1920s, hundreds of Ford's Model T automobiles were rolling off the assembly line every day. America was surely a land of opportunity and progress. Cities were growing. Factories were producing more goods than ever before. Herbert Hoover, who would become the thirty-first president of the United States, said in 1928 that Americans were on the verge of "banishing poverty from the nation."

He was wrong.

America was home to thousands of wealthy families in the 1920s. However, many more American families—millions, not thousands— were poor. Newspapers and movie newsreels rarely told their stories or printed their photographs. They were the farmers who borrowed money from banks. They were the workers in the factories and the mills. Some were immigrants who had just arrived in this country. Others were the sons and daughters of immigrants who had come to America years earlier. Life was hard. Still, most people dreamed of better times to come.

Advertisements in newspapers and magazines and on billboards persuaded people to buy whatever they wanted—cars, clothing, radios, even a house. If the people did not have the money now, they could pay later. And so families bought on credit and installment payments. The profits from all these purchases went into the pockets of the wealthy, while wages for the workers remained low. A gap had always existed between the wealthy and the poor. But in the 1920s, the gap was growing wider. The magic was about to end.

"Did the thought ever enter our bone head that the time might come when nobody would want all these things?" Will Rogers wrote in one of his newspaper columns. People still wanted all the wonderful products America's factories produced. They simply couldn't buy or borrow anything more. Warehouses began to fill up with unpurchased goods. The number of Model Ts rolling off the assembly lines slowed.

Trouble doesn't happen overnight. It swells, like a balloon, one breath at a time. People don't always notice the balloon growing larger and larger. Then one day the balloon bursts. That is what happened in America on October 29, 1929.

On that Tuesday morning in New York City, a crowd had gathered in front of the New York Stock Exchange building. The building was like a palace with six towering pillars. Inside, the walls were marble. On the ceiling were thin layers of gold paint. Here was where Americans—both the rich and those who dreamed of getting rich quick—spent money. They bought stocks, or pieces of paper that gave them a small piece of ownership in a business. Some people bought stock in coal companies. Others bought stock in the cotton and steel industries. Some people had no money to purchase the stocks. And so they borrowed the money just as they had when buying their automobiles and homes. Borrowing money to make money is called "speculation." If someone purchases $500 of stock in an electrical company, that value might increase to $600 or $700 in a few weeks. Then the person makes a profit. But values of stock do not always go up. They also go down. When that happens, the investors lose money. Many such investors in 1929 had no way of paying off their loans.

On that overcast autumn morning in New York City, rumors swirled through the narrow streets like wind. Something had gone terribly wrong. The stock values weren't just dropping. They were crashing. America's banks and businesses were losing money. By afternoon ten thousand people had jammed the streets and sidewalks. Some had climbed onto the statue of Alexander Hamilton outside the stock exchange building because it was the only space left to stand and wait. A reporter for the *New York Times* described the crowd as "wild-eyed" with fear. Men wept. A few days ago they had been wealthy. Now they were penniless.

America's financial balloon had burst. The day would become known as "Black Tuesday." The effects of the stock market crash rippled across all of America. Even those families who had no investments in the stock market suffered. Factories laid off workers or shut down completely. Without a job, families who had bought cars and radios and houses on installment plans could not make their payments. They lost their homes. Even those people who had managed to save a little money in their local banks lost it when the banks themselves closed. Some families fell apart. Thousands of adolescents became vagrants, roaming the countryside. In New York City, Chicago, and San Francisco, breadlines stretched for blocks as the homeless and hungry waited their turn for a free bowl of soup and a heel of bread.

The magic was gone. The Great Depression had begun.

In 1928, President Hoover had predicted that poverty would vanish from the nation. Four years later another president took the oath of office. In his speech to the American people that day, the new president, Franklin Delano Roosevelt, said, "This great Nation will endure as it has endured, will revive and will prosper. . . . The only thing we have to fear is fear itself—nameless, unreasoning, unjustified terror. . . ." Then President Roosevelt made a promise: He would free the American people from their fears.

FDR addresses the nation over the radio. The president promised to free Americans from their fear of poverty.

THE FIELD INVESTIGATOR

Franklin Roosevelt declared a sort of war on the Great Depression. He had a plan of attack, called the New Deal, to end the depression. The New Deal created a number of government-run programs to provide relief to the hungry and homeless and to create jobs that would put Americans back to work.

The Federal Emergency Relief Administration, or FERA, was one of the president's new programs. The director was Harry Hopkins. He hired and trained a team of field investigators. The investigator's job was to travel to small towns across America and document the difficulties of ordinary people. In this way, the government could better understand the problems the people faced and how best to solve them.

Martha Gellhorn was twenty-six years old when a friend of her family introduced her to Harry Hopkins. Hopkins had already hired fifteen field investigators for FERA. Most of those men and women were experienced writers. Martha Gellhorn was not experienced. Perhaps Harry Hopkins saw something in her that convinced him she had the ability to get close to people where they lived and to communicate their stories. Perhaps the friend who introduced Martha to him had pressed Hopkins to offer her a job. Whatever the reason, Martha Gellhorn became Harry Hopkins's sixteenth field investigator.

One of her first assignments was visiting the small town of Gastonia, North Carolina. What Martha saw there she would not soon forget.

In Gastonia, as in other regions of the country, the economic depression had set in motion a vicious cycle: Less demand for products meant less profits. To increase profits, the mill owners reduced wages and increased hours. If the workers protested, they lost their jobs. Most did not protest simply because there was no other work to be had. And so the workers accepted the lower wages, even though this meant they might not have enough food to feed their families.

Day after day, Gellhorn visited the homes of the mill workers. She interviewed them as well as the mill bosses. She learned from the workers that two or three women fainted each day in the mill. The mill bosses denied it, but Gellhorn herself had seen young girls who should have been in school working at the cotton looms without rest for eight hours. They ate their lunches of brown bread while standing in front of the spinning spools. They ate, Martha observed, without taking their eyes off the machines. In a mill bathroom Martha discovered three women lying on the concrete floor. They told her it was the only

Martha Gellhorn.

Martha returned to Washington feeling "flat and grim." Her job was not yet done. She had to write a report for Harry Hopkins on what she had seen. To write about Gastonia was difficult, but not because the place was hard and mean. Martha was simply overwhelmed by the pages of notes in her book and even more so by the images inside her head. She was also angry. The mill owners, in her opinion, were "a bunch of loathsome ignoramuses."[1]

In the homes of each mill worker she visited, she noticed a photograph of President Roosevelt hanging on the wall. In some homes the image was just a newspaper clipping. "The President won't let these awful conditions go on," said one woman. "He's got such good eyes," said another, "he must be a kind man."

At this moment, writing her report, Gellhorn was the president's eyes. How could she make Harry Hopkins—and the president—see what she had seen? Harry Hopkins sent his investigators into the field with this piece of advice: "I don't want statistics from you. I just want

place they could rest for a few minutes without the mill boss shouting at them.

Because Martha worked for the government, the mill owners opened their accounting books so she could see that the mill was losing money. The numbers in red ink did not convince Martha. More upsetting to her were the red sores she saw on the children's legs as she watched them come and go from the factories. The town had no buried sewer pipes. Instead, the runoff from outhouses puddled downhill toward the mill workers' only source of drinking water.

your own reactions, as an ordinary citizen."

And so Gellhorn began to write, dating the report November 11, 1934:

> I came in today from Gastonia. . . . The price of food has risen (especially the kind of food they eat: fat-back bacon, flour, meal, sorghum) as high as 100%. It is getting cold; and they have no clothes. . . . These men are in a terrible fix . . . faced by hunger and cold, by the prospect of becoming dependent beggars—in their own eyes: by the threat of homelessness, and their families dispersed. What more can a man face, I don't know. You would expect to find them maddened with fear; with hostility. I expected and waited for "lawless" talk; threats; or at least blank despair. And I didn't find it. I found a kind of contained and quiet misery; fear for their families and fear that their children wouldn't be able to go to school. ("All we want is work and the chance to care for our families like a man should.") But what is keeping them sane, keeping them going on . . . is their belief in the President. . . .
>
> These people will be slow to give up hope; terribly slow to doubt the President. But if they don't get their jobs; then what? If the winter comes on and they find themselves on our below-subsistence relief; then what?

She ended her report emphasizing again the trust Americans had placed in their president: "Between them and fear, stands the President. But only the President."[2]

Martha was idealistic and strongly opinionated. In November 1934, she wrote to Harry Hopkins, "It would make me happy to send in a report, just once, something rosy to say." But she found nothing cheerful to write about. The job was wretched, she admitted, and eventually she quit.

The stories Martha had written for Harry Hopkins were factual, but they were not news articles. Martha Gellhorn was not yet a journalist. Still, her work as a field investigator had taught her skills that every good journalist must have: keen observation, good listening skills, and patience. Perhaps the most important lesson she learned was to trust her own eyes and voice and to write honestly about what she had seen.

THE PHOTOGRAPHER

In San Francisco photographer Dorothea Lange was luckier than most. Well-to-do families still came to her studio. They sat while Dorothea took their portraits. She positioned their heads and hands. She adjusted the lamp to light their faces. Then she snapped their photographs. Later, in the darkroom of her studio, she developed the film. The customers returned for their framed portraits, which they hung on the walls of their homes. Now that bad times had gotten worse, however, fewer people were knocking on Dorothea's studio door. Even so, she had a comfortable home, and her children had plenty to eat.

As a field investigator in the 1930s, Dorothea Lange traveled through rural America, photographing people who were down on their luck.

One morning as Dorothea stood at her studio window, she saw a man on the corner below. He appeared down-and-out and uncertain of where he was. He looked left. Along that street was the business district. Then he looked right. In that direction was skid row, the poor section of town. There, homeless people slept on thin mattresses on the floors of empty buildings called "flophouses." Again the man turned, this time looking behind him toward the warehouses along the waterfront. Dorothea wondered: *What will he do? Which way will he go?*[3]

As Dorothea watched from her window, a realization came to her. She was not hungry or homeless. And yet she felt as if she, too, was standing on a corner in her life. For a long time she had been unhappy. Inside her studio, each day was the same as it had always been. Outside, however, lives had begun "to crumble at the edges." Not far from where she lived was the White Angel breadline, named after a wealthy woman who provided the daily handouts. Dorothea's customers warned her, "Don't go there!" Those people were beggars, the riffraff of society, they said. To walk among them was dangerous. That morning, however, Dorothea could no longer ignore the sorry condition of those people wandering the streets. She had to *do* something. She took her camera and for the first time went into the street among the hungry and homeless people.

She took many photographs that day. One showed an old man with a dented tin cup waiting his turn in the breadline. His back was to the others. His crumpled hat shadowed his eyes. His face was unshaved. Hands clasped, he leaned upon a fence rail, staring at nothing. After developing the photograph, Dorothea tacked it to her studio wall. Her wealthy customers asked, "What are you going to do with that thing?"

In the studio Dorothea controlled everything—the light and the poses of the people. The portraits were staged; the background, artificial. In the street she controlled nothing—not the light or the way the people stood and stared. The outside world was real. She knew the photograph of the old man had been "worth doing." She thought it might even be important. As for what was she going to do with it, she told her clients, "I don't know."[4]

One day a friend visited Dorothea in her studio. He saw the photograph of the old man on the breadline and other photographs she had taken of the "riffraff" in the streets. The photographs were "valuable," her friend said. He knew a magazine that might be interested in publishing them. It was not a popular or pretty magazine with stories about heroes,

17

criminals, or society families. Instead, *Survey Graphic* published articles about social welfare problems. The magazine purchased one of Dorothea's photographs. It showed a man at a microphone speaking to a crowd in the streets. He was not a Vanderbilt or a Ford. He was just an ordinary man doing something he believed was important: helping people in need. The magazine enlarged the photograph so that it took up the entire page.

That photograph caught the eye of a government worker named Paul Taylor. He called Dorothea and offered her a job with a relief agency based in California. Like Martha Gellhorn, Dorothea Lange would be a field investigator. She would travel through rural areas and report on what she found. Instead of using words, however, she would use her camera to capture the experiences of America's homeless and hungry.

Dorothea was a city girl. "I didn't know a mule from a tractor when I started," Dorothea said. On the road she saw the effects of poverty and drought. Abandoned cabins leaned sideways as if blown by the wind. The roofs had caved in. The wooden siding had curled away from the frames. She saw farmers working with wooden hoes. Their clothes were frayed and patched. She saw men sitting on the porch steps of a country store in the middle of the afternoon. They had no jobs, no land to farm.

After months in the field Dorothea had learned more than just how to tell the difference between a farm animal and a piece of machinery. She learned about courage. "Real courage," she said. "Undeniable courage."[5]

"Ragged, hungry, and broke" was how one magazine described the people Dorothea Lange photographed. This tent is where a family of eight lived.

THE PEA-PICKERS' CAMP

In March 1936, Dorothea was going home. She had spent the past month photographing farm laborers in California. Those weeks had been cold and rainy. On the car seat beside her was a box containing rolls of exposed film. Once back in San Francisco, she and Paul Taylor would develop the photographs and send the prints to Washington. She thought not of her work now but of her children. If she drove for seven hours without stopping, she would be home with her family by nightfall.

Rain fell steadily. Dorothea focused on the road ahead. She had said once that her power of observation was quite good. Her training as a photographer enabled her to see, or at least sense, what was to the right or to the left or sometimes even behind her. It happened again that day. She saw a "crude sign with a pointing arrow." As her car sped by, she had only a moment to read what it said: PEA-PICKERS' CAMP. Dorothea drove on, but her thoughts began to beat back and forth in rhythm with the windshield wipers.

Dorothea, how about that camp back there? What is the situation there? Are you going back?

Still she drove on in the rain. Whoever was living in the pea-pickers' camp was likely no different from the people she had already photographed. During her weeks on the road, she had shot rolls of film. She did not need any more photographs. It was raining. Her equipment was packed away. She was tired and wanted to go home.

Twenty miles later, however, she turned the car wheel and bounced off the road, making a U-turn. She later stated that she was "following instinct, not reason."[6] Something, she knew not what, was drawing her back to the pea-pickers' camp.

At the sign she pulled off the highway in the direction the arrow indicated. "I was following instinct," she said, and her car was a "homing pigeon."

There were many people in the camp, but Dorothea approached only one—a mother. She was sitting just inside a tattered lean-to tent. She held an infant. Her other children, including a teenager, were around her as well. Dorothea saw desperation in the woman's face. She also saw something more: strength.

Dorothea took her time, as she always did in the field. Sometimes she simply sat on the ground and let the children come to her, let them touch her camera. She never slapped their hands away, not even when they were dirty; and they were always dirty. Sometimes she

Dorothea Lange's photograph, simply called "Migrant Mother," captured the desperation many women felt during the Great Depression. This mother struggles to shelter and feed her children.

asked for a drink of water and then purposely sipped it slowly. In the field she had learned how to "slide in on the edges," she said, how *not* to call attention to herself. If the people asked who she was or why she was there with a camera, she told them the truth. She worked for the government, and the government was interested in their troubles.

This day at the pea-pickers' camp the mother did not ask who Dorothea was or why she had a camera. Nor did Dorothea ask the woman her name. They were strangers to each other. And yet the woman told Dorothea some things about herself. She was thirty-two years old. Her seven children ate what they could find—frozen peas in the field and birds the children could catch. Her car had no wheels. Sold 'em, the woman explained, for food.

Dorothea snapped her first photograph from a distance. Then she stepped closer. She took a second, then a third shot. In one image only the mother and her infant are in the frame. The mother holds the child to her breast.

Years later, looking back on this day, Dorothea said she felt as if the work she was doing was important. Her photographs really could help these people in some way.

Perhaps the migrant mother in the pea-pickers' camp understood this as well. Dorothea believed that she did. "She seemed to know that my pictures might help her and so she helped me. There was a sort of equality about it." The mother did not turn Dorothea away. She allowed her to come even closer.

The final shot, the one Dorothea would later caption simply "Migrant Mother," showed the woman sitting with the infant in her arms. Two other children lean upon her shoulders, their backs to the camera. The woman's expression and her fingertips lightly against her cheek express what Dorothea herself had begun to understand: Poverty is tragic but not shameful. The woman was desperate but not defeated.

Dorothea packed her Graflex camera away and got back into her car. The entire session had taken only ten minutes. She shifted into gear and steered through the soggy field for the highway and home.

Dorothea Lange's photographs during the Great Depression helped to create a new type of communication called "photojournalism." These were not portraits of families. Nor were they advertisements. They were social and political images, a new way of seeing America and Americans. The photographs did not illustrate a news story. Rather, they *were* the story. This type of photojournalism would become an important means of communication during the Second World War.

THE SOB SISTER AND THE SERIOUS
NEWSWRITER

Martha Gellhorn and Dorothea Lange did not know each other in the years they worked as field investigators, one on the East Coast and the other on the West. Their work did not appear in newspapers or magazines. It wasn't news. Instead, it was a record of everyday life for the homeless and the hungry. Martha's reports and Dorothea's photographs were research that became part of the government files on the Great Depression. And yet the field investigator's work was a turning point for women like Martha Gellhorn and Dorothea Lange. It allowed them to investigate topics ordinarily not open to women writers and photographers in the 1930s. Social and political problems were the business of men, or so society believed. Women's topics usually focused on caring for children and the home, on fashion and beauty and health.

The Great Depression gave women journalists, too, the opportunity to cover social and political topics. Adela Rogers St. John worked for the *Los Angeles Examiner*. She wrote quite a different story about the people affected by the Great Depression. The newspaper's publisher was William Randolph Hearst. He encouraged his newswriters,

most often his female writers, to "go and find out" what was shocking or sensational, then write about it in a way that might bring tears to the eyes of his readers. Fancy writing was the stuff of novels. He wanted none of that. Rather, his news stories were simply told and full of emotion. This type of writing was called "sob stories," and the women who wrote the stories were called "sob sisters."

Adela's assignment differed from Martha Gellhorn's and Dorothea Lange's. Instead of investigating what life was like for the country poor, she intended to investigate the charities that were supposed to be helping the poor. Her approach differed as well. Many sob sisters went "undercover," pretending to be someone else in order to get a story. Adela's disguise was a thin cotton dress and a frayed coat. No doubt, her shoes were scuffed and run down at the heels. Her own shoes would surely have given her away. These clothes were a costume, borrowed from a movie studio. On a December morning she left home with only a dime in her pocket.

Sob stories often involved a sensational situation. Thirty years earlier, for example, reporter Nellie Bly had pretended to be insane so as to

be admitted to the women's asylum on Blackwell's Island in the East River and later reported the shocking conditions in the *New York World* newspaper. Adela hoped to uncover some shocking details for her newspaper readers as well.

For two weeks Adela wandered the streets of Los Angeles. If anyone asked her name, she replied, "May Harrison." The dime lasted one day. She had spent a nickel on coffee and a roll and the rest on a meager supper. She had no place to sleep. The only mission she knew that took women was completely full. And so she walked. She walked long after store lights went out and the streets were empty. She tugged on car doors parked along the

streets and at last found one that was unlocked. She curled up on the backseat and slept.

She went to employment agencies in the city—always walking because she had no money for the trolley. The agencies turned her away. They had no work. Exhausted, her feet throbbing, she sat at a lunch counter and ordered something to eat. When she admitted she had no money, the restaurant owner served her anyway. It was her first experience with kindness from a stranger.

After two weeks she returned home and wrote her story in the "sob sister" style, full of emotion and melodrama: "Oh Lord help me to walk with bleeding feet," she

THE INVERTED PYRAMID

In March 1932, at two o'clock in the morning, the telephone rang in Ishbel Ross's New York City apartment. The night editor at the *Herald Tribune* apologized for getting Ishbel out of bed in the middle of the night. He needed her *now*. He had just received a news flash–someone had kidnapped the young son of Charles Lindbergh.

Ishbel snapped awake. Charles Lindbergh was the famous aviator who had flown solo across the Atlantic Ocean. This wasn't just news. This was front-page news.

Less than an hour later Ishbel was in a car provided by the newspaper. The driver transported her to the Lindbergh home in Hopewell, New Jersey. In the middle of the night hundreds of news reporters and photographers had likewise descended upon the small town. Each pushed forward, trying to speak with someone—a police officer, a state trooper—who might provide answers to the news reporter's most important questions; called the "five Ws" in journalism: Who? What? Where? When? Why?

Ishbel didn't sleep that night or much of the next day. She worked quickly, gathering facts. Then she wrote the lead paragraph for her article. In a single sentence she identified the essential facts: "The attention of millions all over the world was centered last night on the fate of the infant Charles A. Lindbergh Jr., who was kidnapped from his crib on Tuesday night as he lay sound asleep in the nursery of his home on his father's estate near Hopewell, N.J."

The lead, or first, paragraph is the most important element in a news story. It includes at least two or more of the five Ws. The paragraphs that follow provide additional details that usually explain "how" the news event occurred. This method of summarizing the most important facts in the lead paragraph, followed by supporting details and background information, is called the "inverted pyramid."

The serious newswriter, like Ishbel Ross, focused on the facts in constructing the inverted pyramid. The writing was objective, without emotion or personal opinion. The goal of the news story was to inform the audience about what had happened.

In contrast, the sob sister usually did not follow the inverted pyramid structure. She exaggerated facts and sometimes invented details to weave into her story. The writing was subjective, loaded with emotion. Details about what the characters wore or how they behaved were meant to provoke sympathy from the readers for either the victim of the crime or the villain. The goal of the sob sister story was to entertain as well as to inform the audience.

THE FRONT-PAGE GIRLS OF THE 1930S

On a summer day in 1910, a twenty-two-year-old woman stood in the newsroom of the *New York Herald Tribune*. Desks crowded the room. Paper was everywhere—on the tabletops, in the wastebaskets, and on the floor. Lights blazed. Telephones rang. Typewriters clacked. A reporter shouted, "Boy!" At once a copyboy ran to the reporter's desk. His job was to run errands, most often carrying the typed carbon copies of a reporter's story to one of the rewrite men across the room.

Emma Bugbee was comfortable in a room full of desks and noise. She had been a high school teacher. However, the editor led her out the door and up the stairs to another floor entirely, where the women worked. Things were a good deal more quiet here, but that was not the reason Emma was not allowed to work in the newsroom. She was a woman, and as a woman, her assignment was to write women's news, not the hard news that makes up the front page of a newspaper. Few women wrote front-page news in 1910. Yet even those who did rarely got a desk in the all-male newsroom.

By the mid-1930s, the newsrooms had changed very little. Desks still shouldered one another. Paper clutter was everywhere. Telephones still rang and typewriters still clacked. Copyboys—not girls—still ran errands among the desks. More than twelve thousand women held jobs on newspapers in the mid-1930s, a great deal more than twenty years earlier when Emma Bugbee sat down to write her first women's story. And yet the newsroom was still predominantly a sea of male faces. No more than two or three women worked as front-page newswriters. Some newspapers had no front-page girls at all.

Ishbel Ross was one of the few front-page girls. The front-page girl, she said, was in love with her work. She moved confidently through the streets to investigate riots, fires, murders, and catastrophes. Back at her typewriter, she worked with "lightning speed" to put her thoughts into words. When on an assignment, the front-page girl didn't eat or sleep until the story was done and she could cry, "Boy!" to send her copy to the rewrite desk. She was usually exhausted, Ishbel said. But the job itself was thrilling. The work itself was more exciting than seeing her "byline," or name, printed at the top of the article on the front page.

After writing stories for four years on the *Herald Tribune* staff, Emma Bugbee got her first byline. A year later the editor brought her downstairs into the newsroom. She was at first a novelty, but Emma Bugbee had staying power. As a front-page girl, she would cover news throughout the Great Depression, the Second World War, and the decades that followed.

wrote. "Listen to the cling-clang-clang of the trolleys, 'I'll be all right if my feet hold out.'"[7]

Editors expected their sob sisters to write with feeling and at times to even slant the facts a little. Even so, these types of assignments gave women the opportunity to cover important events.

Not all newspapers published such sensational stories, and not all women reporters were sob sisters. Emily Hahn wrote a story for the *New Republic* that also investigated the plight of women during the Depression. She did not hide her identity as a reporter. She did not dress in costume. Instead, she interviewed welfare workers and volunteers at the YWCA. She approached women in the streets and in the missions—when she could find them. She asked them questions. Afterward she wrote her story with objectivity, not sentimentality:

> There are many women, no doubt, who struggle along until the last possible moment. . . . She tries everything else first, for . . . to admit failure is still the greatest shame of all. She lives as long as possible on her savings. . . . It is not until she is reduced to actual hunger that the white-collar girl at last presents herself at the door of the relief bureaus and charity committees.[8]

Although Emily Hahn was a serious newswriter and not a sob sister, her story was still told from the woman's angle. The woman's angle focused on the human interest element in a hard news story. It was that slice of the story that editors believed women were interested in reading. For example, if the news event was a kidnapping, the woman's angle might be on the mother's anguish over her lost child. Emily Hahn took an otherwise hard news event and reported it from a woman's angle.

The field investigator, the photographer, the sob sister, and the serious newswriter—these were the roles women writers played during the Great Depression. Each woman documented the crisis in her own way. First Lady Eleanor Roosevelt believed in the power of women to make change happen for the better. "We are going through a great crisis in this country," she wrote. "The women have a big part to play if we are to come through successfully."

During the Great Depression, Eleanor Roosevelt herself would play a key role in changing the lives of women journalists. She did something that few First Ladies had ever done. She opened the doors of the White House and invited the ladies of the press inside.

> **The toughest part of a woman's work in Washington journalism is to get a job."**
>
> ★RUBY BLACK,
> JOURNALIST

Chapter Two

THE QUIET
BEFORE
THE STORM

Hard news stories focused on often violent and grim events—murders, fires, bank robberies. Many editors and a good deal of society, too, believed a woman's spirit was too fragile to write about such harsh happenings. They did not have the mental skills required to interpret news; women, or so society believed, were emotional and sympathetic and therefore better suited to soft news and the "sob sister" angle.

Women who sought to make a place for themselves in newspaper work have found editors prejudiced against them," said Stanley Walker.[1] As the editor of the *New York Herald Tribune*, Stanley Walker had seen the work of many young newspaperwomen. Most who landed their jobs were "slovenly," he said. They didn't check their facts. Others were giddy show-offs who hoped to gain fame from their sob sister stunts. Others simply weren't good writers. They had gotten their jobs on their good looks or, more likely, through connections—someone who knew someone else who asked an editor for a favor.

No doubt, there were also male newswriters who were slovenly show-offs. But the newsroom was a man's world in the 1920s and 1930s. The few women who entered and failed unfortunately made it all the more difficult for the skilled women reporters to be taken seriously. Ishbel Ross was different, said Stanley Walker. The toughest assignment never upset her. She had a logical mind. She wasn't giddy. She was, he said, "the man's idea of what a newspaper woman should be."[2]

Yet even when women like Ishbel Ross had proven to be excellent journalists, they still faced roadblocks. They were not always welcomed in newspaper circles. By 1933, Ruby Black had been writing serious news for two decades. Still, she often felt as if she was on the outside looking in. "It is years, usually," she said, ". . . before other newspaper men give [a woman] tips and ask her for information in the way they trade with their male colleagues."[3]

In Washington, DC, the National Press Club banned women journalists from membership. Nor were women invited to the many White House press briefings. This type of female exclusion was called "skirting," a reference to women's clothing. Skirting happened in other places besides the newsroom. Women could not enlist in the military and so could not fight as soldiers for their country. In the world of music, men rather than women conducted orchestras. Nadia Boulanger was an exception. When she led the Boston Symphony Orchestra in concert in 1938, *Time* magazine wrote a story about her remarkable achievement.

"When Mrs. Roosevelt swept into the White House like a strong April breeze," said Ishbel Ross, "she blew the cobwebs of tradition out the window, invited the [ladies of the] press upstairs, showed them where the President slept, let them look at him having his tea, and generally made them feel that they were welcome."[4]

The First Lady did more than give the ladies of the press a tour of the White House. She created the Monday-morning press conference.

No First Lady had ever held weekly press conferences. Mrs. Roosevelt was the first, and she insisted that only women reporters could attend.

MONDAY MORNINGS AT
THE WHITE HOUSE

On a winter day in 1935, Frances Lide took the two hundred dollars she had saved while working for a small newspaper in Greenwood, South Carolina, and boarded a train for Washington, DC. The Depression had hit the news industry hard. Many newspapers had gone out of business. News was always happening in the nation's capital, however. Frances hoped to land a job working for a large news bureau.

Soon after she arrived at Union Station, bad luck struck. Someone stole her luggage. With no clothes other than what she was wearing, Frances desperately needed a job. She found her way to "Newspaper Row" on Pennsylvania Avenue. Here within a few city blocks were the offices of the *Washington Star*, the *Washington Daily News*, and the *Washington Herald*. Surely one of these big-city newspapers needed a reporter.

Frances's bad luck continued. Although the young reporter from South Carolina knocked at every newspaper door, no editor would even see her. But Frances Lide was not about to give up. It was a long train ride back to Greenwood. She devised a plan.

On a Saturday night, she returned to the offices of the *Washington Star*. She knew the city editor and his staff would be "putting to bed" the stories for Sunday morning's edition. The newspaper's secretaries, however, would not be working. Frances just might be able to slip past their empty desks to knock on the city editor's door. Her off-hours visit paid off. The city editor saw her. By Monday afternoon Frances knew she had a job. Later she learned that the editor had called a local gentleman whose name Frances had provided as a reference. The editor asked him, "Is she the type of reporter who 'lets her petticoat show'?"

The gentleman had answered, "I'm sure she does not." [5]

A petticoat is a lady's undergarment. To "let your petticoat show" meant writing like a woman—in other words, not checking the facts or writing with too much emotion. Frances got her job, in part, because she didn't let her petticoat show and, in part, because she was ambitious enough to keep trying. She also got the job because her luck had changed. The First Lady's secretary had just announced that no men could attend the Monday-morning press briefings. Mrs. Roosevelt did not want to compete with the president and his press coverage, her secretary explained. FDR would cover national and international news. Mrs. R's stories would be social, not political. And so, said the secretary, only ladies of the press were invited.

The First Lady had another motive. She intended to "give women news that men could not get." By closing the door to men, Mrs. Roosevelt had opened a door for women. For years the United Press news service, or UP, had resisted hiring women. Now the UP hired Ruby Black to represent it each week in the White House. Likewise, Frances Lide's assignment for the *Washington Star* was covering the First Lady's press briefings.

On a December morning Frances walked for the first time across the portico of the White House. An usher wearing white gloves opened the door for her. Inside, another usher checked her name off a list. She waited in the Green Room on the first floor with the other women. Among those gathered was UP reporter Ruby Black.

At eleven o'clock the usher entered. "All right, ladies," he said, and lifted the red velvet rope.

The women bolted forward and up the Grand Staircase to the second floor. This was the private living area for the president and his family. Reporter Ann Free recalled that a few of the elderly ladies "elbowed" her out of the way in their rush down the corridor to the Monroe Room. Those who arrived first usually claimed a chair in the front row. Frances found a seat toward the back of the room. Those who arrived last sat on the floor.

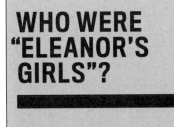

WHO WERE "ELEANOR'S GIRLS"?

Twenty to thirty reporters usually attended Mrs. R's Monday-morning press conferences. They could be classed into one of three groups:

● The first-string news girls: They wrote news stories, many of which were front-page news. They had the ability to write and think fast. Facts were the heart of their stories.

● The feature writers: Features were articles about unusual or interesting people and events. These women added colorful or emotional anecdotes to their stories. They usually got a byline.

● The women's page writers: Food and fashion were the most frequent topics in the women's page department. But increasingly in the 1930s, women also wrote about current affairs. Mrs. R's weekly press conferences provided plenty of story ideas.

"Good morning, girls!" the First Lady's high-pitched voice trilled as she entered the room with her two secretaries. "Hello, hello, hello," she repeated as she moved around the room, shaking the hand of each reporter. This routine was how Eleanor Roosevelt began each press session. "I don't think Mrs. Roosevelt ever knew my name," Frances said. "Yet she shook my hand once a week."[6]

The First Lady carried a black notebook, bound with rubber bands. This was her calendar. Once everyone had settled in their chairs, she undid the rubber bands and opened the book. She reviewed her engagements for the week. Questions and answers came next.

Some days Mrs. Roosevelt brought a guest. In 1935, flying ace Amelia Earhart answered questions during the press conference. Other days Mrs. Roosevelt presented her views on social issues that concerned her. Ending child labor was one of those topics. Poisonous cosmetics was another. She passed around the room photographs of a victim who had been blinded by a product called Lash Lure. She had found the photographs in the files of the Department of Agriculture. "I cannot bear to look at them," she told the girls, but she urged them to write stories about the dangers of chemicals used in cosmetics.[7]

The story on this particular winter day, however, was the remodeled kitchen in the White House. A hotel-size electrical stove and ovens were the highlights. Frances Lide took notes as she toured the kitchen with the others. The stove was made of stainless steel and spotless. The kitchen walls were cream colored. A border edged the new linoleum floor.

The *Washington Star* had an afternoon deadline. Frances had to write her story that same morning. She read and reread her notes. "I was new to Washington and really didn't have a hard news background," Frances said. "I probably wrote more things than were necessary."

Finally, after three hours, she walked into the press room with the article. An editor read it, folded it in half, and pushed the papers through a sharp spike on his desk. Frances might have been new to Washington, but she knew what that meant. A "spiked" story was one an editor considered not important enough to publish.

Frances had failed, but not because her story was sobbing with emotion. She had not shown her petticoat. Her story was accurate with lot of details. It just wasn't . . . news.

In Greenwood, South Carolina, the newspaper for which Frances had worked before coming to Washington had a staff of two people. In the nation's capital Frances learned that newspaper work was a competitive business. Martha Strayer worked for the *Washington Daily News*, which also had an afternoon deadline. Because their newspapers were competitors, so too were Martha and Frances. During the weekly press conferences Frances watched anxiously as Martha scribbled notes using a system of rapid handwriting called "shorthand." Symbols that looked like swirls and half circles replaced words and phrases. Frances simply could not keep up. "I used to be petrified as to what Martha was writing in all those notes," she said.

Martha's talent, however, was more than just the ability to take notes quickly. She knew how to angle a story to grab the readers' attention. Stories with an interesting angle or slant often escaped the spike. One Monday morning, for example, Mrs. R reported that the White House had been inspected for electrical defects. That afternoon the *Daily News* ran this headline: WHITE HOUSE FIRETRAP.

Mrs. Roosevelt had not used the phrase "firetrap." But that was the way Martha Strayer had slanted the story. Frances remembered what happened in the pressroom of the *Washington Star*: "My editor called me over and said, 'You didn't write that.' I said, 'I certainly did. They just threw it away.' It happened to a lot of stories I'd turn in on Mrs. Roosevelt. . . . Somebody in the news room would look at that and think, 'Well, they're just working on the electrical system,' and put it on a spike. . . . It wasn't important enough, the way I wrote it."[8]

Frances had landed a job with a big-city newspaper. But she still had a lot to learn about writing the news.

THE PEACEFUL YEARS

In her autobiography *This I Remember*, Eleanor Roosevelt called the time between 1934 and 1936 "the peaceful years." The phrase was misleading. True, the world was at peace, but on the horizon were war clouds. These threats of war had been darkening for two decades, ever since Germany surrendered to the Allied forces in 1918, ending the First World War. Ten million men from many nations had died during four years of fighting. Cities had been bombed into ruins.

Adolf Hitler was an Austrian who fought for Germany in that First World War. Gas grenades had wounded him physically. Weeks later Germany's surrender wounded him emotionally. This second wound ran very deep and never healed. The terms of the surrender had shamed the German people. The victors placed harsh demands on Germany. They reduced its military and did not allow an air force. Territories Germany had proclaimed or conquered as its own were now returned or given to other countries—France, Poland, Czechoslovakia. The German people were to pay for rebuilding the foreign lands they had bombed. Perhaps the worst demand of all, at least in the wounded mind of Adolf Hitler, was that Germany accept all blame for the war and the ten million dead.

Adolf Hitler vowed revenge. Although indignant, he was patient. His plan would take years. In 1925, he wrote a book that he called *Four and a Half Years of Struggle Against Lies, Stupidity, and Cowardice*. His publisher advised him against that long title and suggested instead *Mein Kampf*, which translates in English to *My Struggle*. Hitler belonged to the National Socialist Party, also known as the Nazi Party. In his book he explained how the Nazi movement would restore Germany to its former glory. He had two goals: one, to acquire by force lands to the east taken from Germany via the 1918 surrender treaty; and two, to destroy the Jewish people. These people, he wrote, had betrayed Germans. During hard economic times they prospered. They soiled German blood by marrying Germans. In Hitler's mind the Jewish people were evil, and he urged them to leave Germany while they still had the chance.

Dorothy Thompson was a young American writer living in Berlin, Germany, at the time *Mein Kampf*

Adolf Hitler salutes the ranks of Hitler Youth during a parade in 1935.

Ten years ago:

THE NAZIS BURNED THESE BOOKS

...but free Americans CAN STILL READ THEM

Once Germany declared war on America, the Office of War Information created posters like this one to educate Americans about the threat the enemy posed on their everyday freedoms.

Hitler might one day rule Germany? Dorothy Thompson read *Mein Kampf.* The hateful statements against Jews particularly disturbed her. She wanted an interview with the author. In 1931, Adolf Hitler agreed to meet with her.

Dorothy was nervous as she waited in the lobby of the Kaiserhof Hotel, the location of the Nazi Party headquarters in Berlin. Suddenly, she spied Adolf Hitler hurrying to his room. Bodyguards surrounded him. She believed Hitler would become the future leader of Germany. If she was correct, then an interview with him was an important news story.

Within seconds of entering Hitler's room, however, Dorothy felt she had been wrong. His behavior was not what she had expected from a powerful leader. Throughout the interview, he did not look directly at her. At times his voice rose almost to a scream. He was physically short and seemed small in other ways

rolled off the presses. She was the first American female journalist to head a news bureau in Europe. She wrote stories about world leaders and politics for the *New York Evening Post.* In the 1920s, Adolf Hitler was not yet a world leader. He was not even well liked, even in Germany. Most people dismissed his book, *Mein Kampf,* as nonsense, the published ravings of a bitter and unstable mind. However, as Adolf Hitler and his Nazi Party gained power in Germany, public opinion changed. Was it possible that as well. Soon after the interview Dorothy Thompson wrote a book titled *I Saw Hitler!* In this book she described the German Nazi leader as "insignificant." She wrote: "He is formless, almost faceless. . . . He is the very prototype of the Little Man . . . the eyes alone are notable. Dark gray . . . they have the peculiar shine which often distinguishes geniuses, alcoholics, and hysterics."[9]

In *Mein Kampf,* Hitler had written that physical fitness was "more valuable" to the Nazis and to Germany than "intellectual weaklings." Dorothy Thompson could not help thinking that Hitler himself was such a weakling. In her book she wrote, "I bet he crooks his little finger when he drinks his tea." She left the hotel that day with the conclusion that the world had little to fear from this insecure man.

Sigrid Schultz was also an American newswoman living in Berlin. She, too, headed a news bureau, the only other woman besides Dorothy Thompson to do so at this time. Because Sigrid worked for the *Chicago Tribune,* she and Dorothy were competitors. Sigrid also managed an interview with Hitler. During their meeting he had shouted, "My will shall be done!" Sigrid's opinion of the Nazi leader was very different from Dorothy's. Hitler was a man to fear.

NEWS SERVICES AND BUREAU CHIEFS

A news service is an organization that gathers and distributes news stories. News publications subscribe to news services. Editors select which stories their publications wish to publish. The Associated Press and the United Press are two examples of news service organizations. These news services were also called "wire services" in the past because they transmitted their stories via telephone and telegraph wires.

A news bureau, on the other hand, is an office where news stories are written and transmitted to its members. In the years before the Second World War, American newspapers as well as the news services had offices, or news bureaus, in many European cities, including London, Paris, Berlin, and Vienna. The bureau chief not only oversaw the news stories but also worked closely with the newswriters.

In the 1930s, Sigrid Schultz and Dorothy Thompson headed news bureaus in Europe. Dorothy Thompson was the Berlin bureau chief for the *New York Post,* while Sigrid Schultz headed the Berlin bureau of the *Chicago Tribune.* The two women were often rivals for the same news stories.

In 1933, students carrying Nazi flags march around the bonfire of "un-German" books in Berlin.

The Nazis paid close attention to the foreign journalists in Germany and to what they were writing about Hitler and his rise to power. Sigrid was just five feet tall, but the Nazis referred to her as "that dragon from Chicago."

Sigrid knew the Nazis were watching her. At night she was careful when driving her car. She had heard stories of how the secret Nazi police had rammed cars off the road. Even so, she didn't miss a deadline. She continued to write and file her stories. The Nazis continued to watch her closely, but they did not interfere with her work. [10]

Germany elected Adolf Hitler into power the same year that Americans voted Franklin Delano Roosevelt into the White House, 1932. These two leaders could not have been more different, not only in appearance but also in beliefs. They led their people down two opposite paths. Although these paths went in different directions, they would one day cross.

Within weeks of taking office, Adolf Hitler dissolved the existing German government. He censored the press. He formed a new secret state police force called the SS. In March 1933, the first enemies of Hitler marched through the gates of the newly constructed Dachau concentration camp. In May the book burnings began. Thousands of people, many of them teenagers and university students, gathered in public squares. They heaped books onto the bonfires. The words of novelists, historians, and even scientists whose views did not agree with Hitler's curled and crackled in the flames. All books written by Jewish people were burned as well.

In 1934, Dorothy Thompson returned to Germany. She traveled by automobile through the country toward Berlin. Three years had passed since she had interviewed Adolf Hitler. Germany had changed significantly. In villages new Nazi flags hung from every house. A black swastika blazed against a bloodred background. "They made the streets look very gay, as though there were a festival," she said. She estimated that one million flags were flying over Germany.

As she drove, she came upon a Hitler Youth camp. A very large banner with a swastika painted on it "stretched hillside," she said. It read: YOU WERE BORN TO DIE FOR GERMANY. The children were beautiful, she said. They wore uniforms

Two dictators, Benito Mussolini, who ruled Italy, and Adolf Hitler, who ruled Germany, ride together in an open car in this photograph from the late 1930s.

DOROTHY THOMPSON

Dorothy Thompson was born on July 9, 1893, in Lancaster, New York. Her father was a reverend. Her mother died when Dorothy was just seven years old. The care of her younger brother and sister became Dorothy's responsibility until her father remarried two years later. At nine years old Dorothy was outspoken, a quality her stepmother disliked.

When she entertained, the stepmother often brought Dorothy into the parlor to curtsy to the ladies gathered there. One day, instead of bowing politely as a proper girl should, Dorothy did a cartwheel. The guests, six members of the local Methodist church, were mortified by the sight of Dorothy's underpants.

Dorothy was always a little rebellious. When she was a child, her father often punished her misbehavior by making her memorize passages from books on his library shelf. Being forced to read was not really a punishment. Dorothy loved it.

Eventually, her stepmother convinced the reverend to send Dorothy away to live with an aunt in Chicago. Years later, when asked about her childhood, Dorothy described it as unhappy.

In high school Dorothy's tomboyish ways continued. She became captain of the basketball team. Although she still loved to read, she didn't care much for studying and school rules. She graduated and began her college studies at Syracuse University. Friends there remembered Dorothy as someone who liked to talk. She often monopolized everyone's conversations.

Beyond basketball and

and sang songs. The air rang with their voices. But the camp frightened her. Dorothy pressed hard on the gas pedal and shifted into gear. "I wanted only to get away from there," she said. [11]

Had she stopped and investigated more thoroughly, had the Nazi leaders allowed her to get close, she might have found even more disturbing images: the hide-and-seek games the children played in which the strongest boys pummeled the weakest—the youth leaders looked on but did nothing to stop the beatings. She might have seen the wrestling matches or the field combat exercises and how those who had succeeded humiliated those who had failed. She might have heard the lyrics to the banner song the children sang so beautifully:

We will keep on marching
even when everything
falls into ruin
Because today Germany

books, Dorothy soon developed a new passion: writing. She traveled to Europe in 1920 with the intention of becoming a journalist. She had an ability to be at the right place at the right time and so get "scoops," or stories, that no one else could. She interviewed a political prisoner in Ireland who later died on a hunger strike. In 1935, she began interpreting news rather than reporting it. "I don't like reporting," she once said. "I like ideas." Soon her ideas began appearing three times a week in a column called "On the Record," published by the *New York Herald Tribune.*

Outspoken as a child, Dorothy was equally outspoken in her newspaper column. She warned the world of Hitler's power. Some people in the newspaper world called her a "blue-eyed tornado." Others called her an "American Cassandra." Cassandra was a character in Greek mythology who always predicted terrible things to come. Even so, by the beginning of the Second World War, Dorothy was one of the most widely read columnists in America and one of the highest-paid writers. In 1938, she earned more than $100,000 for her newpaper column, radio broadcasts, and speaking engagements.

After the Second World War, Dorothy's influence on public opinion was not as powerful as it had been before and during the war. She also took an unpopular position when she suggested that the German people were not totally to blame for Hitler's brutality. Some newspapers dropped her column because of this viewpoint.

Dorothy Thompson died of a heart attack in Portugal in 1961.

belongs to us, tomorrow
the whole world.

Heinz Beck was one of those Hitler Youth who attended the camps. He played the war games and sang the songs. "Adults and elderly people must have shuddered when hearing this," he wrote many years later. "But they could not interfere. Parents were not allowed to speak up."[12] Some parents feared saying anything against Hitler and his policies because the Hitler Youth had been trained in the camps to turn in their friends and family for treason.

Arriving at last in Berlin, Dorothy checked into the hotel where she had always stayed. Even here, she learned more about the changes Hitler had imposed upon his people. His secret police had executed hundreds of political leaders without giving them a trial. Those killed had opposed Hitler and his policies. Alone in her hotel room, Dorothy Thompson understood that she had made a serious mistake in 1931. She had underestimated Adolf Hitler and the power of his Nazi Party.

The next morning an SS agent knocked on her door. "He was a young man in a trench coat like Hitler's," Dorothy said. "He brought an order that I should leave the country immediately." [13]

Dorothy had committed no crime. However, she had mocked the führer in her book *I Saw Hitler!* She had called him a small man of no consequence. Apparently, Hitler had read the book. No American journalist, male or female, had ever been forced to leave Germany. Dorothy was furious and refused to leave at first. But then the American ambassador to Germany warned her she had better do as Hitler ordered. Germany had changed, he argued. She was no longer safe in this country.

"I packed my things and went downstairs," Dorothy said.

A porter helped her with her luggage. "Auf Wiedersehen," he said in German, meaning "Come again soon." But as long as Hitler was in power, Dorothy Thompson could never return to Germany.

At the train station Dorothy faced still another surprise. Her male colleagues—reporters for wire services, radio networks, and newspapers; in fact, just about *every* foreign correspondent work-

ing in Germany—had gathered on the platform. They gave her a bouquet of long-stemmed red roses. Their appearance at the train station was risky. The powerful Nazis were surely watching and could have punished them as well with expulsion. Dorothy cried as she boarded the train, but not because she was frightened. She was moved by their show of support for her. Being female didn't matter anymore. She was one of them.

Hours later, when the train arrived in France, reporters were there to interview her. Hitler kicking her out of Germany had made front-page news!

Dorothy Thompson was not the only person who had underestimated Hitler. In fact, in the years to come, many world leaders, including the future prime minister of England, Neville Chamberlain, would view Hitler as dangerous but not a threat to the world. Still, Dorothy was determined not to make the same mistake twice. She intended to fight Hitler and Nazism the way she knew best—through her political column called "On the Record."

Back home in America, she wrote about Hitler, warning that Germany was preparing for war, but the rest of the world seemed not to know or care. She wrote about Benito Mussolini, the dictator of Italy. His Fascist army invaded the small African country of Ethiopia in 1935-1936. She wrote about Emperor Hirohito, whose Imperial Japanese Army invaded China around a year later. She wrote about the frenzied people who donned uniforms and blindly followed these dictators. The Nazis of Germany wore brown shirts, she wrote. The Fascists of Italy wore black shirts. They argued in cafés, shouted in the streets, and published newspapers declaring they were superior to all others. They would create a new world order.

"Nazism . . . Fascism . . . Totalitarianism . . . ," she wrote. "For the sake of these words and what they represent, bombs fall; yesterday in Ethiopia, today in China and in Spain, tomorrow—where?" [14]

Dorothy Thompson was not the only journalist writing about dictators in Europe, but she was one of the most widely read. Originally hired to write the woman's point of view on political matters, her columns surprised many readers, including her publisher. She did not limit her interpretation of politics to women's issues. She wrote of world leaders and governments. She wrote passionately of injustices, but she was no sob sister. She rooted her opinions solidly in facts. Her years of living in Europe and running a news bureau gave her credibility. They gave her something else, too: sources! She quoted poets, bankers, dictators, and presidents—all of whom she had met personally.

Soon newspapers across the country were carrying Dorothy Thompson's column. Readers—both men and women—folded open the page where Dorothy's column appeared. "When Dorothy Thompson goes out and digs up a story she almost always gets her facts right," *Time* magazine wrote in 1939. "She appeals to men because, for a woman, she seems surprisingly intelligent." Women in small cities and towns especially admired her, *Time* reported. She was successful and independent—the kind of woman they wanted to be. [15]

For certain, not all readers agreed with Dorothy's point of view. Many community leaders thought her a warmonger, someone who wanted the United States to declare war on Germany. In the 1930s, Americans were still struggling to defeat the Great Depression. So what if Italians wore black shirts and paraded behind Mussolini? So what if Hitler Youth were singing patriotic songs? And even if those Nazi children grew up to become Nazi soldiers, that still did not concern them. After all, two broad oceans separated America from the rest of the world. The storm would never reach America's shores.

"LIKE HOUSES WITH THE SHUTTERS DOWN"

On an autumn afternoon in 1936, Anne O'Hare McCormick sat on the White House porch, sipping iced tea with the president of the United States. Franklin Roosevelt rarely granted interviews with news reporters, but Anne was different from most. For one thing, she didn't take notes. She said note taking made people nervous. Instead, she listened and watched and studied small details. The president enjoyed chatting with her, he said.

Anne O'Hare McCormick was not one of Eleanor's girls. Like Dorothy Thompson, she was a political columnist. When hiring her, the *New York Times* editor had given Anne this most unusual assignment: "You are to be the 'freedom' editor. It will be your job to stand up on your hind legs and shout whenever freedom is interfered with in any part of the world." [16] Anne had proven herself to be so good at her work that the *Times* appointed her to its editorial board. She was the first woman journalist in America to receive such recognition.

Anne had recently returned from Europe. She had interviewed Adolf Hitler and Benito Mussolini. What she had seen and heard troubled her greatly. She had much to stand up and shout about in her news column, "Abroad."

"The face of the world has changed," she wrote. "You walk familiar streets and they are strange. People everywhere are like houses with the shutters down, withdrawn and waiting, as if life were held in suspense; or," she added, "they are quarreling within their houses, hating one another because long-drawn-out uncertainty has rasped their nerves to the breaking point." [17]

No doubt, Anne "chatted" that late afternoon with the president about what she had seen in Europe. Especially troubling for her were the ways the Nazis were persecuting the Jewish people. Signs that read JEWS NOT WANTED were in café windows. They could not attend the theater or motion pictures. "Customers are photographed coming out of Jewish shops," she reported. "Even old friends are afraid to visit or speak with them."

Compared to "the murky atmosphere" of Europe, Anne thought America seemed "light and clear." She gazed across the White House lawn. Through the trees, she could see the Washington Monument. The evening had grown cool. A servant

In 1937, Anne O'Hare McCormick became the first woman to win journalism's highest award–the Pulitzer Prize.

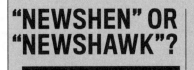

"NEWSHEN" OR "NEWSHAWK"?

When *Time* magazine referred to Anne O'Hare McCormick as a "newshen," the magazine received a letter of complaint from Edith Snyder Evans. She was a news reporter for the *Knoxville News Sentinel* in Tennessee. Labeling a women reporter a "newshen" was downright insulting Edith said.

"If anything," wrote Evans, women had to be "more newshawkish" in order to compete with their male colleagues. What infuriated Edith even more, however, was that *Time* had tagged Anne O'Hare McCormick in such a degrading way. Any reporter who managed to interview Benito Mussolini in Rome was definitely a hawk, not a hen.

Time published the letter in its February 3, 1936 issue. But the magazine did not change its policy. Throughout the 1930s and 1940s, *Time* (as well as other periodicals) continued to refer to women journalists as "newshens."

ANNE O'HARE McCORMICK

Anne Elizabeth O'Hare was born in England in 1882. Her parents were Americans. Soon after Anne's birth the family returned to the United States and settled in Columbus, Ohio. When Anne was fourteen years old, her father abandoned the family. While Anne was still in school, her mother supported her children by working in a dry goods store. She had also written a book of poetry called *Songs at Twilight.* She earned a little extra money by selling copies of her book door-to-door.

After Anne's graduation from St. Mary's Academy the family moved to Cleveland. Here, both Anne and her mother worked for a weekly Catholic newspaper.

At the age of thirty Anne fell in love with a man eight years older than her and married him. Francis McCormick was a businessman who traveled throughout Europe. Anne accompanied him. She loved meeting and talking with people. She often wrote in her journal about the friends she had made and the places she had seen. In the 1920s, she wrote to the managing editor

brought jam sandwiches. Two Irish setters slept at the president's feet.

The American president seemed hardy and healthy and completely relaxed despite the war clouds across the Atlantic. The bad times of the Depression were slowly getting better. Still, the president spoke that night about the work that still needed to be done. Americans had not yet regained their sense of worth. He was confident that evening, however. As Anne listened to the president, she felt herself begin to relax too.

Columnists like Dorothy Thompson and Anne O'Hare McCormick do not gather news in the same way as a reporter in the street does. A columnist *interprets* news. Soon after her visit with the

president, Anne explained to the readers of her column the difference between the dictators in the world and the American president: Dictators, she wrote, acted alone. They ruled the lives of millions of people, and these people had no voice, no power to question the dictator's orders; the American president led rather than ruled millions of people. He acted in cooperation not only with the Congress and the courts but also with those people who had elected him to the White House.

The women who covered Mrs. Roosevelt's press conferences were not political columnists like Anne O'Hare McCormick and Dorothy Thompson. They had never seen Hitler or Mussolini or Hirohito

of the *New York Times* and asked if she might not send him some stories about the people and the political situation in Europe. His answer was simply, "Try it."

Soon the *Times* was publishing Anne's stories in a column titled "Abroad." She interviewed dictators. She also interviewed and wrote about ordinary people affected by the brutal power of dictators. In 1936, she won the journalist's highest honor: the Pulitzer Prize. She was the first woman journalist to do so. She earned another unique distinction by becoming the first woman to sit on the editorial board of the *New York Times*.

She died at the age of seventy-two on May 29, 1954. The *New York Times* ran a black border around her column as a sign of mourning. A few months before her death, she had written about the power of women. They had a responsibility, she said. They must see to it that America's moral and spiritual values remained strong.

She wrote: "Women, and particularly American women in a time when the United States is thrust into a position of unique power and influence, have the soul of the nation in their keeping." [18]

except perhaps in movie newsreels. Nevertheless, they questioned the First Lady: Was force the only way to handle the present difficulties in Europe and the Far East? If war came to Poland, to France, or to England, would America also fight?

These were not soft news questions on household innovations. These were hard-boiled political questions. Mrs. Roosevelt had promised not to focus on such international issues, as these were the president's business. Still, it was a promise hard to keep. She told her "girls" that they, too, had "a special stake" in watching national and international news. "Every woman should have a knowledge of what is going on," she said. [19]

And so she shared with them details about her recent visit to England, which was bracing itself for war with Germany. Children there were learning how to wear gas masks. If war came to England, she commented, would it not also come to America? The ocean that Charles Lindbergh had crossed in 1927 could no longer protect Americans. The fighter planes of the Luftwaffe—the German air force—could cross that ocean. "It is time for us to decide," she told her news girls, "whether this civilization of ours is worth preserving, or whether we might as well let it go." [20]

Eleanor Roosevelt was also sounding the alarm. The peaceful years were over.

> **"The scene of the refugees around the station was the most horrible I had ever seen, worse than the refugees in Poland. Fortunately, there was no bombing. Had there been any attacks it would have been too ghastly for words. Children were crying. There was no milk, no bread."**
>
> ⭐SONIA TOMARA, *NEW YORK HERALD TRIBUNE*, JULY 14, 1940

Chapter Three

REFUGEES
AND PARTISANS

"Blitzkrieg" is a German word that means "lightning war." The British and Americans reduced it to a single, chilling syllable: "Blitz." Blitzkrieg was Adolf Hitler's war strategy. It involved both surprise and speed.

The German führer assured the leaders of the world that he had no intention of going to war. He signed peace pacts with some countries. Then, in a series of deliberate and swift maneuvers, his armies attacked. Overhead, hundreds of German planes darkened the skies. They dropped parachute flares that triggered fires on the ground. The light from the flames guided the bombers to their targets. On the ground a new type of German tank called a "panzer," lightweight and fast, rolled through fields, crossed rivers, and surrounded cities. Germany had begun building the panzers years earlier, calling them "tractors." But Hitler never intended these armored vehicles to plow fields.

First Poland fell to the Nazis' Blitz. Then Czechoslovakia, Denmark, and Norway. Each victory came quickly, before the opposing armies could muster a powerful enough defense. The Nazis overran the Netherlands. Belgium, too, fell within days. Hitler's intention to rule all of Europe was now brutally clear.

People fled from the Nazi troops who occupied their countries. Thousands of refugees crossed the border of Belgium into France. Surely they would be safe here, they thought.

German troops parade through Warsaw, Poland, in 1939.

53

France had the greatest military in the world. Its ally was England. The British had sent troops to France to fight the Nazis. In June 1940, however, desperate news reached Paris: The Nazis had broken the French line of defense in the Ardennes Forest. The French and British armies were in retreat, and Hitler's troops were marching toward the capital. Now the people of Paris became refugees. They fled in panic.

These frightening events made headlines in newspapers in England and in America. A handful of American women newswriters were living in Europe during this time. They had a front-row seat to these breaking news stories. They were in the thick of it. Hitler's conquest of Europe was the biggest story of their lives. How could they not write about it?

Virginia Cowles was living in Paris as a foreign correspondent for the *Sunday Times*, a newspaper published in London, England. She fled the city with the other refugees and later wrote about the experience. Cars and trucks and bicycles— anything with wheels—clogged the roads. The air was thick with the smell of gasoline. People shouted at one another to get out of the way. Some cursed. Others cried. Some people who had no automobiles or whose vehicles had broken down gathered their small bundles and walked. Those too old or too exhausted to go farther simply sat on the side of the road, not knowing what to do.

Along the road a bakery van ran out of gasoline. The van blocked the road. The cars behind the van honked their horns. People shouted at the woman driver, who pleaded with them to give her some gasoline. Virginia watched as three men got out of their own cars and together pushed the van off the road into a ditch. Virginia later described what happened in an article she wrote for her newspaper. "The rear axle broke and the household possessions piled on top sprawled across the field," she wrote. The woman "flung herself on the ground and sobbed." No one cared. No one stopped to help her. [1]

Sonia Tomara also fled Paris. She estimated that five million people swarmed the roads of France. So great was the number of refugees that the French army had difficulty getting military supplies to the front lines. The people pushed forward, heading south toward Bordeaux and the coast. The great majority did not know where they might end up. They knew only that they must escape the certain dangers of living under Nazi rule.

Within a few days, Sonia had made her way to Bordeaux. The Nazis were not here—at least, not yet. Still, the news was grim. Military leader Charles de Gaulle had fled the country for England. France was on the eve of surrender. The next morning Sonia sent a story to the *New York Herald Tribune*. A blanket like a dark cloud seemed to cover the city, she wrote. The people were not excited or angry. Rather, they felt hopeless. They walked through the streets dazed, without looking at one another, as if they were robots. They sat in restaurants and cafés because they had nowhere else to go. [2]

In the cafés the people listened to the radio broadcasts. One afternoon soon after Sonia had arrived in Bordeaux, the people heard a military officer state over the radio that the French army could not stop the Germans. "It is with a heavy heart," the French officer spoke, "that I tell you that we must try to stop the fight."

Defeat had come to France. Sonia looked around. Tears were in everyone's eyes.

Photographer Therese Bonney wears the medal of the White Rose of Finland, which that government awarded to her for bravery under fire.

THE TRUTH RAIDS

When the Nazis invaded France in May 1940, General Weygand of the French army supplied Therese Bonney with a car, gasoline, and papers naming her an official photographer for the military. A car and gasoline were valuable materials during wartime. That a woman should receive these goods plus documents allowing her to travel with soldiers to the front line was most unusual. But then, Therese Bonney was a most unusual woman.

She didn't plan to become a photographer. When she was a college student in America, Therese imagined herself a professor of languages. She could speak four foreign languages, including French and Spanish. After graduation, in approximately 1920, she traveled to Paris to continue her studies at the famous La Sorbonne university, where she earned her doctor of letters degree. Afterward she did not return at once to America. Instead, she became involved with a project started by the American Red Cross. The First World War had recently ended, and cities and villages throughout Europe were still in ruins. Therese began working to provide relief for children throughout Europe who were victims of this terrible war. Relief included distributing clothing and food to orphans whose parents had been killed. It also included the operation of nurseries, schools, and

playgrounds. Therese never forgot the suffering she saw during those years. Children were the hope of the future, she believed. But children were also the most vulnerable victims of war.

Therese remained in France. She had always admired photographs, though she had never used a camera herself, and she had a knack for organizing art exhibits. This led eventually to her decision to create her own business—a picture news service. She hired photographers to hunt down news stories and supply photographs. She then sent these photographs to newspapers in thirty-three countries. Increasingly, she became unhappy with the photographs others were taking, so she picked up a camera and began hunting news stories herself.

Pictures could reveal as much information as the written word. People from different countries who spoke many different languages could still read and understand a photograph. So instead of becoming a professor of languages, Therese used her pictures as a way to speak to the whole world. She called her photographic expeditions "truth raids."

The Nazi Blitz in France was not the first time the American had risked her life to photograph war. In Finland she had hidden from enemy planes by burying herself in snowbanks. Her heroic efforts to document Finland's fight against the enemy had earned her that country's highest honor, the Order of the White Rose. Now she pinned that medal to her jacket as she followed the French troops to the banks of the Meuse River in the Forest of Ardennes.

Across the river was the German army. Overhead, German Stukas, or dive-bombers, flew just above the treetops and strafed the French troops. When the French troops retreated, a seemingly endless line of panzers crossed the river in pursuit. Throughout the fighting and the retreat, Therese Bonney focused her lens and shot.

Others had photographed battles and dead bodies, she once said, but those images had not stopped the killing. Therese's truth-raid images were different and often surprising. In one photograph a cow stands in a field. In the background panzers roll toward it. A cow in a field

In 1943, Nazi SS troops forced Jewish families at gunpoint from their homes onto trains. The families had no idea that their final destination was concentration camps, where many would not survive.

on a summer day is expected; a war machine is not. In this single frame Therese had captured the symbols of war and peace. The cow is unaware of the death and destruction approaching across the field.

In another frame she focused on a spiderweb of telephone lines. The severed lines showed clearly that the Nazis had silenced the voices of France.

On June 22, 1940, after just six weeks of war, France surrendered. Although Therese Bonney had lived in France for many years, she was still an American citizen. Germany had not yet declared war on America, and so Therese was in no immediate danger. Still, she booked passage on a ship bound for America. She arrived home armed with photographs. They would become her weapons of war.

In the United States, Therese Bonney exhibited her photographs in museums and libraries. She gave public lectures. She wanted Americans to see and hear what she had seen and heard. She exhibited her photographs in New York at the Museum of Modern Art. Those who saw the photographs were both surprised and saddened. Writer Archibald MacLeish called them "eloquent" and "moving." They were all the more powerful, he said, because the people were anonymous. They were not the leaders of armies. They were not soldiers. They were ordinary citizens caught in the nightmare of war.

As a result of the exhibit, the Carnegie Corporation awarded Therese Bonney a grant to continue her work. "I'm the only woman who went to this war with a gun—a flash gun," she told a reporter with a smile. And she was going back.

But why? the reporter asked. Why risk your life for the sake of a few photographs?

Therese tried to explain. She was not a photographer, she said. She was a historian. The camera was just a tool she used to capture the truth and bring it back for others to see. She wanted to show what war does to ordinary people. "The living men, women and children . . . are what counts," she said. [3]

"It is hard, hard, work—bristling with risks—lucky if you come out of it," Therese admitted. But her truth raids were "a magnificent chance to contribute your brains and talent to a great cause, the world's." [4]

Therese Bonney was going back to war to fight for peace.

Therese Bonney's photograph of a cow grazing while German tanks approach suggested the violence and hardship that war would bring to Europe during the war.

SHADOW LIVES

After surrender came occupation. First the soldiers arrived, often in tanks or goose-stepping (a type of march) through the streets. Then came the Gestapo, the secret police of the Nazis. Hitler had specific tasks for them: to enslave the "inferior races" and to crush any resistance to Nazi rule, using whatever means necessary. The Gestapo rounded up the rebels and either tortured them into revealing the whereabouts of other rebels or sent them away to concentration camps. The widespread arrest of Jewish people followed. The Nazis forced many into cattle cars and shipped them to the camps. Others, they simply shot and shoveled into mass graves.

To prevent resistance, the Gestapo closed churches and universities; they arrested priests and professors. They shut down movie theaters or allowed only German films to play. Nazis ran the newspapers and the radio stations. In Germany in the 1930s, the Nazis had taken control of the press and so controlled the information the people received. They did the same thing in Poland and the other countries they occupied. In doing so, they created a Nazi version of history and of current events.

Over a radio broadcast from England, French General Charles de Gaulle made a plea to his people— both those who had escaped to England and those who had not: "Whatever happens, the flame of the French resistance must not and shall not die." Listening to such broadcasts was illegal under Nazi rule. The Gestapo might severely punish anyone caught with a radio.

At first the people in Nazi-occupied countries had little choice but to cooperate with their captors. They obeyed orders. They stepped aside when German officers moved into their homes or onto their farms. The "inferior races" worked in the factories and the fields, then watched as the Germans took what they had made or grown. They carried identification papers and produced them whenever a Gestapo agent demanded to see them. They were off the streets by 10:00 p.m.

In time, however, the women, the men, and even some of the children created shadow lives. During the day they appeared obedient. At night they organized into secret groups intent on resisting the Germans. The simplest form of resistance was hiding a radio and tuning in to broadcasts from the

Partisans, or underground resisters, risked their lives to fight the Nazis, who had occupied their country. Julia Diamant Pirotte was a Jewish partisan in France.

free world—the BBC in London and the Voice of America. Many more took greater risks.

Marie-Antoinette Morat was a resister, a partisan. She helped to print and distribute the underground paper *Combat*. She did more. She gave up her identification papers, and therefore her name, so that a Jewish girl her age could avoid capture by the Gestapo. She took a new name, Lucienne Guezennec. The resistance forged new identification papers for her.[5]

At first the word "resistance" was not used, said Lucienne. "Friends who knew my anti-German feelings asked me to do a few 'errands,'" she explained. "I was elated. I felt like a new Joan of Arc. At last I could do something."[6]

The "errands" might include sabotage, or the deliberate destruction of factories, rail lines, or communication facilities. Anything that delayed, disrupted, or destroyed an enemy mission was a way of fighting back. Smuggling information about the resistance movement was equally important. American reporter Tania Long lived in London and wrote for the *New York Times*. Her story "The Free Press of Enslaved Europe" described the heroic efforts of people who risked their lives to print underground newspapers. Her story also reported on the vengeance of the Gestapo officers who captured these resisters. In the following passage she describes the execution of a resister called "H.C.": "The stillness of the gray dawn is shattered by a shout of 'Feuer.' A volley of shots rings out, a body falls. People still asleep in the neighborhood shiver and draw their blankets closer as if they have just seen something evil in their dreams."[7]

Many more people, she reported, were quietly arrested and whisked away to concentration camps. "Yet however many may disappear," Tania wrote, "there are always more to take their places. And when the Nazis succeed in crushing underground papers, others spring up like mushrooms after a summer shower." In every Nazi-occupied country, resistance cells organized. The Gestapo had ways of learning the identity of those with shadow lives. Often the Gestapo retaliated cruelly. If a partisan killed a German soldier, the Gestapo might torch that person's village or round up a dozen or more men and women and stand them before a firing squad.

Among Tania's sources of information was Andre Simon, though she suspected that was not his real name. After two years he had managed to escape France. In London he described how the Gestapo frightened the French people out of reading underground newspapers. The Germans created hundreds of fake pamphlets and mailed them to a list of French homes.

"Immediately after the mail was delivered, and often before the victim had even had time to open the envelope containing the decoy, a Gestapo agent would enter the home and arrest the recipient for reading illegal literature," Simon told Tania. "Receipt of a faked pamphlet was then excuse enough to send the victim to a concentration camp."

The Polish people secretly printed news sheets. They folded them inside their clothes and passed them from one person to another. These secret sheets of paper, hidden from the Nazis, gave the Polish people hope that help from the free world might one day come. "Despite the very worst," Tania concluded, ". . . the Nazis have not been able to stamp out the free press—their most dangerous opponent in any of the countries they have conquered."[8]

The brutish treatment by the Nazis did not end the resistance. Rather, the blood of the people strengthened it.

EUROPE'S CHILDREN

Although Nazi occupation did not necessarily mean defeat, it most certainly meant hardship and starvation. Especially vulnerable were the children of Europe.

By February 1941, Therese Bonney had returned to the war front. She traveled to England, Sweden, Portugal, Spain, and France. In each country she risked her life to capture photographs of those who suffered. She focused her camera most frequently on children. Many months had passed since the Nazis had conquered and occupied the countries of Europe. The change in Therese's viewfinder was shocking.

Two years earlier children on their way to school had smiled into her camera. They wore clean white stockings and polished shoes. They sat at their school desks with book and pencil, eager to learn. Now the white stockings were gone. Instead of playing in schoolyards, they huddled in doorways begging for food.

Dirty and hungry, children carry empty sacks through a field, hoping to salvage something–if only a few rotten oranges–to eat. Therese Bonney took this photograph in Spain.

REVIEWS OF *EUROPE'S CHILDREN*

One of the great books of this war is the work of a photographer. . . . This is a picture book about war and oppression, without a battle scene or soldier, without bombs or planes or ships. It is a book, moreover, in which the camera proves more powerful than the pen.

★BRUCE DOWNES,
PHOTOGRAPHY,
DECEMBER 1943

Miss Bonney braved death again and again to collect this account of what war is doing to the younger generation in Europe. More than anything I've yet seen, it makes one understand what the Nazis mean when they talk about eliminating their neighbors by malnutrition.

★WM. PHILIP SIMMS,
SCRIPPS-HOWARD
NEWSPAPERS, MARCH 1944

Look at these pictures some quiet evening at home. You will be seated . . . in an overstuffed chair. . . . You will hear the radiator purring and your healthy children will be making ready for a soft, warm bed. . . . Look at these pictures and see if you *dare* close the book without a prayer.

★H. C. G., *AMERICA,*
MARCH 11, 1944

In Spain she raised her camera and framed three children, a boy and two girls. Mud caked the girls' bare legs. Over their shoulders were canvas sacks. The trio stood with their backs to the camera. The field before them was barren. There was no food.

In France she photographed the door of a bakery. Boards blocked the entry. Printed in French across the boards were the words *Plus de pain—inutile d'insister:* "No bread—useless to insist."

The photographs were important because no one had focused on the children before, not in this way. Therese Bonney had not posed the children or used phony backdrops.

Her photographs had captured life as it truly was.

Some photographs she captioned. "They climb to would-be homes in gutted houses," she wrote. "In wind and rain they beg. . . . They search for food and so often all they find is rotten oranges."

The people in America who saw these photographs could not believe the cruelty of the Nazis. And yet the Nazis had stated their starvation policy in public speeches in Germany.

The war orphaned many children. Together they found some comfort and warmth.

Adolf Hitler's policy was to starve those people he conquered so that Germans could live and prosper. Children suffered the most, Therese Bonney said.

Hermann Göring was Hitler's second in command. Göring told the Nazi troops how they were to treat the people in the occupied countries: "You are not sent out there to work for the welfare of the people in your charge, but to get the utmost out of them, so that the German People can live. That is what I expect. . . . It makes no difference to me . . . if you say that your people will starve." [9]

"Whether nations live in prosperity or starve to death interests me only in so far as we need them as slaves," stated another well-known Nazi leader, Heinrich Himmler. "Otherwise it is of no interest to me." [10]

Therese Bonney photographed the horror of war: infants wrapped in paper because there were no blankets; children sleeping on the floor of an orphanage, one curled next to the other; a boy with twig-thin legs sucking his fingers. This was truly the horror of war. And yet she photographed positive images as well: sacks of grain in a village, donated by the American Red Cross; a nun feeding an infant; a boy with a scarf tight around his neck sipping from a bowl of watery soup. His shining eyes reveal his happiness for even just this little.

Therese was fighting for the future of the world—its children. Their situation was horrible but not hopeless. They needed food, clothing, and medicine, and her pictures could help make that happen. She began to plan a book of photographs called *Europe's Children*. She carefully selected each photograph and arranged them in a particular order. Then she wrote a brief introduction: "With my camera I have made this record in France, Spain, England, Sweden and Finland. . . . [These pictures] might have been taken in a score of other countries today. I have written this story with my lens. This is the truth for which I vouch." [11]

Therese submitted her photographs to publishers in the United States. One after another—ten in total—rejected her book proposal. Perhaps they thought the images too shocking for Americans to see. This was Europe's war, after all. America was still at peace. Eventually, Therese published the book herself. She charged three dollars a copy and asked all who were interested to send a check to the National City Bank in New York City.

Something wonderful happened. People who saw the book were haunted by the images. They told others, and they, in turn, bought a copy and then told still others. Book reviewers wrote articles about it. *Time* magazine called it "the war's most shocking book." Soon all two thousand copies Therese had printed sold out. A publisher now stepped forward and offered to reprint the book commercially.

All across America people saw the photographs and shuddered. Many took action by making donations to the American Red Cross. Perhaps the photographs were so effective because people saw in them the eyes of their own children. Could this terrible fate happen to them as well? Therese Bonney's photographs had suddenly personalized the dangers that correspondents like Dorothy Thompson, Sigrid Schultz, and Anne O'Hare McCormick had been writing about for the last few years.

Now they understood. Hitler had to be stopped. But how?

LIFE ON THE RUSSIAN FRONT

In 1936, a new type of magazine appeared on American newsstands. *Life* told news stories in pictures. These were not ordinary photographs of people posing in front of a camera. Instead, they were "photo-reports" similar to those Dorothea Lange had taken of ordinary people struggling to survive during the Great Depression. The magazine sold for ten cents an issue. Each week a new issue took readers on a journey across America and the world. In the first issue photographs showed the construction of the world's largest earth-filled dam in Montana. Another issue showed rescuers delivering food and water to flood victims in Ohio. The magazine took readers into private homes as well, including Thanksgiving dinner with President and Mrs. Roosevelt.

Publisher Henry Luce had hired just five photographers, the best in the country. One of these was a woman, Margaret Bourke-White. Luce had seen her photographs in magazines. Her work was unusual. She photographed towers and bridges, skyscrapers and steel mills, even the inside of a meatpacking plant. Her images were realistic, sharp, and crisp. More than that, she had a way of making ordinary things—like the arches of a railroad bridge—seem like art. She also took risks to get just the right shot. For one assignment, she had climbed the steel girders of a building under construction. Eight hundred feet above the ground, she snapped her photograph.

One of her fellow photographers on the staff found Margaret "bossy." But everyone agreed she was an expert camerawoman. When she was on an assignment, nothing stopped her from getting the photographs she wanted.

Early in 1941, the editors gave Margaret a challenging assignment. They suspected that Hitler's peace treaty with the Soviet Union would prove as meaningless as all the other treaties the führer had signed. They wanted a photojournalist on the scene in case the Nazis invaded that country. And so, a few weeks after Therese Bonney had packed her trousers and helmet to return to war-torn Europe, Margaret Bourke-White packed her camera equipment

Margaret Bourke-White goes to war as an accredited correspondent for *Life* magazine.

and started out for the Soviet Union. She took five cameras, three thousand flashbulbs, and two portable tanks to develop her photographs in her hotel room if necessary. [12]

The differences between these two women photographers were significant. Therese Bonney was not working for anyone but herself. Margaret Bourke-White was on assignment. Therese Bonney traveled alone. Erskine Caldwell, Margaret's husband, traveled with her. The photographs they took differed as well. Therese focused her lens on the victims of war, the children in particular. Maggie, however, was determined to get as close to the front lines as possible and shoot the war itself.

In June 1941, the Nazis invaded the Soviet Union. Just as the *Life* editors had hoped, Maggie was the only foreign photographer in the country at the time. But the American ambassador to the Soviet Union ordered all Americans to leave the country, including *Life's* star reporter.

In the world of journalism, a "scoop" is when a writer or photog- rapher is the first person to cover a news story. The German invasion of the Soviet Union was the biggest scoop of Maggie's life. She sat on the edge of her chair in the ambassador's office and pleaded with him to allow her to stay.

"The loss of life and destruction are bound to be terrible," he argued. "There are still two seats left on the train to Vladivostok; it might be your last chance."

Risk was a part of her job, she argued.

After a few minutes the ambassador reconsidered. "If . . . it is your considered action to stay," he began, "our Embassy will help in every—"

Before he could finish, Maggie rushed forward and kissed him. [13]

MARGARET BOURKE-WHITE

Margaret Bourke-White, called Maggie by her friends, was born in June 1904 in the Bronx, a section of New York City. Even as a child, Maggie did things most little girls didn't do. She loved reptiles and often kept snakes, frogs, and turtles as pets in homemade cages. She wanted to become a herpetologist, traveling the world to study rare snakes. Maggie shared this love of the outdoors with her father, who was an inventor. He often took her into factories. The turning and sparking of machine parts fascinated her.

During her first year of college her father died suddenly from a stroke. Her father had been the most important person in Maggie's life. She was heartbroken. She soon discovered that the family didn't have enough money to pay for her to continue college. She began working at odd jobs to earn enough to finish her first year of college. Her father had loved photography. Somehow Maggie's mother found enough money to purchase a twenty-dollar camera for her daughter. Maggie's initial interest in photography was simply to use it as a way to earn extra money. She still believed she'd become a herpetologist. Eventually, though, the photographs she took for her college yearbook and magazine, even for her fellow students, began to get recognition. Maggie gave up studying snakes and instead focused on photography.

She wasn't interested in photographing people. Rather, she took her camera into industrial buildings and factories. She captured the angles of arches and bridges and the intricate gears of machines, large and small. She entered her photographs in contests and won. *Fortune* magazine, which specialized in stories on business and industry, bought her work. Soon publishers around the country began to see and admire Maggie's photographs. When publisher Henry Luce began a new pictorial magazine called *Life*, he knew he wanted Margaret Bourke-White to be on his staff. Maggie accepted the job.

At the outbreak of the Second World War, Maggie became the first woman correspondent accredited by the War Department. While traveling to photograph the fighting in Africa, Maggie's ship came

On a summer night in June, the first bombs fell on Moscow. Maggie and Erskine were living in a hotel apartment near the Kremlin, the building that housed the Soviet government. Whenever the air-raid sirens wailed, the blackout wardens ordered everyone into the shelters. Maggie and her husband often hid inside their apartment to avoid being forced underground. If she was going to photograph the war, she had to be where she could see it, preferably on her hotel balcony.

under attack. A Nazi submarine torpedoed the ship. She and the other survivors spent a day in a lifeboat before being rescued. Later Maggie would become the first female photojournalist the military allowed to go on a bombing raid with air force pilots.

After the war ended, Maggie continued to travel the world and to photograph news events and news makers. In 1949 she traveled to India. She interviewed the leader of that country, Mahatma Ghandi. This remarkable man, she wrote, believed that even "the atomic bomb should be met with nonviolence." Hours after her interview, an assassin killed Ghandi.

In 1952 she asked her editor at *Life* magazine to send her to Korea, a country that had been at war for two years. While Margaret believed the reporting had been excellent, she felt no one had explored the war's effect on the Korean people. *Life* agreed to her request. She spent months roaming the countryside, talking with and photographing the people. Despite the hardships of war they were friendly, happy people with a wonderful sense of humor.

In May 1961, President Kennedy announced plans to send a man safely to the moon by the end of the decade. Space exploration was a new science in the 1960s. The president's plan was both exciting and challenging. The publisher of *Life* magazine promised to give his star photojournalist the assignment. As soon as the scientists at NASA approved travelers aboard their spaceships, Margaret would get the green light to document the mission.

On July 20, 1969, America succeeded in meeting President Kennedy's challenge. Neil Armstrong was the first human to step onto the surface of the moon. But Maggie never got the opportunity to photograph the mission. She had been diagnosed with Parkinson's disease, an illness of the nervous system, in 1956. Since that time she had undergone two rare operations to ease the paralyzing tremors caused by the disease. The operations were successful, but Maggie's body would never be as strong as when she was younger. In particular, speech was difficult. Still, she managed to write her autobiography, *Portrait of Myself.*

In 1971, she fell while at home. She later died from complications brought on by Parkinson's.

One evening while she was working inside the American embassy, the air-raid siren began. Maggie had plenty of time to go downstairs into the cellar shelter. Instead, she crawled through a window onto the roof of the embassy building. She later described what she saw: "Bombs were falling, and flames began shooting up in scattered spots, giving me pinpoints of light on which I could focus. . . ." She could hear the Nazi planes. Search lights swept across the sky.

It looked to Margaret as if "the whole sky was covered with a luminous plaid design." [14]

Suddenly, the air seemed to change. The planes still droned. The fires still brightened the sky. But instinct told Maggie to find cover. She had just crawled back inside the window and huddled on the floor next to her precious camera when the explosion ripped through the building. The bomb shattered all the windows. Glass "rained down" on her. She was wearing sandals and so slowly stepped over piles of jagged glass to get to the bomb shelter in the basement of the building. Later, once she was safe inside that shelter, she discovered she was bleeding. "My fingertips were cut by glass splinters," she said.

The Blitz continued for twenty-two nights. Each night Maggie set up her cameras on the balcony and waited. The sky seemed "startlingly big," she said. She watched as searchlights sliced the darkness above her. When the bombing started, she was ready. She got her photographs.

Maggie pressed for and finally received permission to move with a Soviet convoy closer to the fighting on the front lines near Yelnya and Smolensk. In this region a battle had raged for weeks. Reports stated that thousands of German and Soviet soldiers had died. While traveling to the front, Maggie did not see long lines of refugees as Virginia Cowles, Sonia Tomara, and Therese Bonney had. The Soviet leader Joseph Stalin had spoken to the people through a radio broadcast. Like General de Gaulle, he told them to resist. Do not run, do not panic; stay and fight underground, he said. Give the Nazis nothing. Scorch the earth, if necessary. Maggie saw the scorched earth. Whole villages had been burned by the villagers themselves so that the Nazi soldiers could not have food or shelter.

Along the way partisans approached the convoy. Maggie listened to their stories. In one village German officers had made a log schoolhouse their quarters. The women had set fire to the building in the night. The soldiers fled from the flames, but the women were waiting outside. They attacked the Nazis with the only weapons they had—pitchforks. [15]

One day Maggie met Tanya. During the day Tanya was a nurse. At night she was a scout for the Soviet cause. She strapped a pistol to her leg. She darkened her face and pulled a cap over her long blond curls. She crawled close to the Nazi camps and listened. Casual comments by a soldier might reveal troop movements or information about weapons. These valuable details she reported to the partisans once she had safely returned.

Long ago Margaret Bourke-White had earned a reputation with her editors for doing more than completing an assignment. She often probed deeper to learn more of the story, especially the stories of ordinary people. She probed deeper now. She asked to go with Tanya on a night mission. A few years later Maggie wrote about that frightening night.

"We were led to the edge of our little wood and told that we could run across an open meadow to another grove of trees about a quarter mile away," she said. First one person, then another started across the meadow. Then it was Maggie's turn. She was only halfway across the open space when suddenly the sky lit up. The Soviet army behind her was firing over her head, and from the other side of the meadow, in the grove, the Germans also opened fire. Maggie did not stop. She ran hard for the safety of the trees. "Even as I ran," she remembered, "I could not help but notice what a brilliant glow the star shells threw on the ghost-white birch trunks." [16]

Maggie made it across the field to the enemy lines. The experience helped her to understand the extraordinary risks the partisans took for the love of their country and for freedom. She safely returned to the camp. It was near midnight, but Tanya had not yet returned. The convoy was preparing to move forward under the cover of night. Maggie would have liked to have waited until dawn to see Tanya one more time. She had no choice, however, but to gather her gear and advance with the convoy. She would always wonder what had become of Tanya.

On the battlefields of Yelnya, Maggie saw the "tattered remnants of life: a torn sleeve, a piece of a boot." And helmets . . . always helmets. The dead had been buried in mass graves. On some mounds were wilted flowers. Artillery had split the trunks of trees, and bomb craters had filled with mud. "The place looked like the end of the world," she said.

In the side of a hill she discovered dugouts used by the German soldiers as bunkers, or shelters, during the fighting. She slipped inside and eyed the dark, cramped space. She picked up a helmet, adorned with a swastika. The name printed inside was HERBST.

Margaret fingered the bullet hole above the left ear. Surely this was how Herbst had died, she reasoned. Soldiers, she had learned, often took helmets or other items from the enemy as souvenirs.

Maggie was not a soldier, she was a photojournalist. But in doing her job, she, too, had risked her life. She believed her photographs were a way of defeating the enemy. As long as people knew the truth about what was happening, they would continue fighting dictatorships. When once again the convoy advanced, Maggie took the Nazi helmet with her.

> The editor sat at his desk. 'I like your stuff,' he said. Then he added, 'But we don't have women on the foreign staff.' Helen Kirkpatrick had heard this before. And she'd hear it again. 'I like your stuff,' said the publisher of the *Chicago Daily News*. 'But we don't have women on the foreign staff.'
>
> This time Helen fired back. 'I can't change being a woman. But you can change your policy.' [1]

Chapter Four

ATTACK
OF THE RISING SUN

Dorothy Thompson, Anne O'Hare McCormick, Therese Bonney—these women correspondents had each lived overseas for a time before the war began. Their knowledge of foreign countries and cultures helped them to land jobs in the newsroom. Helen Kirkpatrick had also lived in Europe before the war. She had begun her career as a string correspondent, or "stringer." A stringer works part-time for a publication, confirming facts and writing stories. In the 1930s, Helen had seen evidence of Hitler's military buildup long before the Nazi panzers had invaded any country. She wrote a book about the troubling times in Europe called This Terrible Peace.

I n 1939, Helen had returned to America to speak about her book. That's when she met the publisher of the *Chicago Daily News*. He liked the book she had written. He'd offer her a job as a foreign correspondent, if she wasn't a woman.

A friend who attended the meeting suggested that other news organizations were anxious to hire Helen. Perhaps that changed the publisher's mind. Or it might have been Helen's refusal to take no for an answer. The publisher did not change his newspaper's policy, at least not officially. But when Helen left Chicago, she was the new foreign correspondent for the *Daily News*.

THE LONDON BLITZ

In 1940, soon after Helen returned to England, the German Luftwaffe, or air force, began bombing London. At night waves of German bombers took off from France and crossed the English Channel. Throughout London, air-raid sirens wailed. People stumbled from their beds and took shelter in what's called the city's "Tube," or system of underground railways. The police and the fire brigade stayed above ground to fight the fires caused by the bombs.

Helen Kirkpatrick did not go into the Tube. Instead, she went to the docks of London on the city's East Side, where dozens of "monstrous" fires raged. She heard the crackling flames, the crash of brick and wood, and the shouts of the firefighters.

The fire brigade was the subject of her story. Even hours later, after she had returned home with pages of notes, the fires burned. "I could have read a newspaper by the [fire]light," she said. "It lit the whole of London. And, of course, [the Nazis] used that to guide planes in and drop more bombs."[2]

The London Blitz continued, night after night. After one particularly long night of bombings and firestorms, Helen found the strength to pedal her bicycle back to her room. She was amazed to discover that despite the bombings, her home was still in one piece. She later described that night as the "most frightening" she had ever experienced. Rather than going to bed, she rolled a sheet of paper into her typewriter. "London still stood this morning," she began. "But not all of London was still there, and some of the things I saw this morning would scare the wits out of anyone."[3]

Hitler had hoped to reduce London to ashes and so weaken the resolve of the people to fight. Helen ended her story by stating that Hitler had failed in his mission. Briton, she wrote, would fight on.

To protect their children from the Blitz, many parents sent their sons and daughters to live with relatives or friends in the countryside. Some children boarded ships bound for America, where foster families would care for them until the war ended. Tied to the buttons of their coats were identification tags. Many children were not so lucky. Bombs had destroyed their homes and left more than a few orphaned.

The Blitz continued through the winter and into the spring of 1941. Then the air-raid sirens fell silent. Days, then weeks passed.

Surely the silence was only temporary. Still, the country sighed with relief. Some children returned to their families.

While the bombing of London had stopped—at least for the time being—war continued to rage in other parts of the world.

In London, photographer Toni Frissell was amazed to see St. Paul's Cathedral still standing amid the ruins caused by Nazi night bombing.

THE WAR IN CHINA

Much had happened to Martha Gellhorn since she had resigned her position with Harry Hopkins and FERA. She had worked for a short time in the White House answering mail for Eleanor Roosevelt. She had written a book about her work as a field investigator. She had traveled to Paris and then to Spain, where she wrote her first war news stories for *Collier's* magazine. While there, she met American writer Ernest Hemingway. He divorced his wife to marry Martha. By 1940, Martha was living with her husband on the island of Cuba.

She listened to the radio for war news from Europe. It sounded "like a funeral," she said. One country after another was falling to the German army. News reports from China were just as grim. Japan was an island nation with few natural resources. China, on the other hand, was a great land mass and rich with resources, including coal and iron. In order for Emperor Hirohito to become a world leader, his country needed China's valuable resources. The emperor took them by force. Japan's "army of the rising sun" had invaded China in 1937. Thousands of soldiers and civilians had died during the previous three years of fighting.

In September 1940, Germany, Italy, and Japan signed the Tripartite Pact, also called the Three-Power Pact. Each country agreed to come to the assistance of the others if attacked by Britain or the United States. On her sunny island Martha Gellhorn shivered. The three dictators—Hitler, Mussolini, and Hirohito—intended to carve the world into pieces for themselves.

When *Collier's* asked Martha to go to China to report on the war, she jumped at the opportunity. She had always wanted to see Asia. This might be her last opportunity. More importantly, she was bored on her island in the sun. Radio news was frustrating. She wanted to see for herself what was happening on the war front.

China was a backward country. The people were very poor. Clean drinking water was hard to find. Sewage streamed in the muddy streets. Diseases like typhoid, cholera, and leprosy were widespread. Martha herself came down with a type of fungus between her fingers. Mosquitoes and flies were a constant annoyance. Martha's Chinese escorts led her on horseback over narrow mountain passes. Cold rain fell steadily, and the wind

Posters during wartime used fear as a persuasion tool. In this poster, produced by General Motors Corporation in 1942, Emperor Hirohito and Adolf Hitler are plotting to conquer the United States.

blew wildly. Martha dusted her bedding with a flea and lice powder, but she was often too cold and too wet to sleep. If a person can be miserable and happy at the same time, then Martha was. Flea-bitten and exhausted, she was nevertheless in high spirits. She was not listening to a voice in a boxed radio. She was in the thick of things.

Martha Gellhorn was not the only foreign journalist in China at this time. Another female correspondent, Shelley Mydans, was also on assignment with her husband, Carl, for *Life* magazine. Martha, however, convinced the Chinese military to escort her to the war front where the soldiers were holding out against the Japanese.

Martha described the Chinese army as a "straggling" and "tattered" band of beggars. Once in formation, however, with their automatic weapons and hand grenades ready, they appeared more "solid" and "self-confident."

79

She thought the rugged mountains were beautiful. The mountains were one reason why the Japanese had yet to conquer China. Military tanks could not easily navigate the muddy trails. Still, the Japanese attacked by air. In the villages bamboo huts with thatch roofs offered no protection from bombs. In one village the air-raid siren was a gong made from parts of an unexploded Japanese bomb.

The Chinese people surprised Martha. "They accept calmly anything that happens: hunger, fatigue, cold, thirst, pain or danger," she wrote in one of the news stories she sent to *Collier's* in March 1941. "They are the toughest people imaginable, as no doubt the Japanese realize."[4] Martha wondered if the Japanese could ever conquer the country.

The United States had long protested the Japanese invasion of China. At the time Martha Gellhorn was in China reporting on the war, the United States had ended all trade with Japan. The Japanese needed American steel and scrap metal to build airplanes and ships and American oil to fly their planes. But the United States refused. The relationship between the two countries had reached a breaking point.

Martha's stories for *Collier's* mentioned nothing about steel and scrap metal or the blistering relationship between Japan and America. Although she was reporting from a country at war, she was not writing war news. Instead, her stories were more like travelogues. No doubt, her readers found them interesting. Martha was an expert at weaving vivid details into her writing. She had learned her lesson well while working for Harry Hopkins. She did not gloss over reality. There was nothing glamorous about flea bites and lice, but that was how life was in China and that was how Martha wrote it. Most likely, the readers of *Collier's* wondered why a woman would risk traveling alone through such an uncivilized country. Martha could have told them. She had three brothers. Her parents had raised her the same way as they had raised them. "Men do whatever they want," she once said. "I assumed I could do whatever I wanted."

After she was home, Martha wrote a letter to her friend Eleanor Roosevelt. In this letter the correspondent expressed her fears for the future. The world was so full of hatred, Martha wrote. She was not alone in worrying about what might happen next. Throughout the summer and autumn of 1941, news editors at *Life* and *Time*, as well as many military officers, began to speculate that Japan was planning to attack American forces somewhere in the South Pacific. No one, however, knew for certain just where or when the next attack of the Land of the Rising Sun would occur.

"WE INTERRUPT
THIS PROGRAM"

On the evening of December 4, 1941, Senator Thomas Connally of Texas gave a radio address. He was speaking to the American people, but his words were a stern warning to Emperor Hirohito. The senator's voice was confident, almost arrogant. That night radio listeners heard the senator say:

> We want no war with Japan. No sensible man wants war anywhere, anytime. But we have precious rights to protect. Our people have rights. I would say to Japan if she is bent upon conquest, if she is bent upon violating our rights . . . if she is determined to have war, I would remind her that we have a navy in the Pacific Ocean, a mighty navy, a navy that knows how to shoot and knows how to shoot straight and strong. I would counsel Japan in all kindness that she had better not seek war with the United States of America.[5]

Even as Senator Connally spoke that night, Japanese aircraft carriers were steaming across the Pacific Ocean. On deck were hundreds of fighter planes. Painted on each wing was a red sun, a symbol of Japan. Emperor Hirohito needed no reminder that America had a navy. And the emperor knew just where to find it: Pearl Harbor, on the island of Hawaii.

Several days later, on a Sunday afternoon, many Americans on the East Coast had just tuned in to a radio broadcast of a football game between the New York Giants and the Brooklyn Dodgers. Sounds of fans cheering could be heard in the background. Suddenly, the radio was silent. And then a voice said, "We interrupt this program with an important bulletin from the United Press." The announcer continued: "Flash! Washington. The White House announces Japanese attack on Pearl Harbor."

The announcement took less than half a minute. The football game resumed.

On another station, just three minutes later, a program featuring the music of Sammy Kaye's orchestra had just ended. An announcer made this statement: "From the NBC newsroom in New York: President Roosevelt said in a

81

statement today that the Japanese have attacked Pearl Harbor, Hawaii, from the air. I will repeat that. The Japanese have attacked Pearl Harbor in Hawaii. . . ."

Throughout the afternoon, the news bulletins continued. They came in fragments between the regularly scheduled programs. Hawaii was not yet a U.S. state, and many people had never heard of Pearl Harbor. Some simply didn't believe the reports.

At 4:15 p.m., a Pittsburgh station reported a few more details. Still, what had happened and why remained unclear. The announcer stated: "We have witnessed this morning the attack of Pearl Harbor and a severe bombing of Pearl Harbor by army planes, undoubtedly by Japanese. The city of Honolulu has also been attacked and considerable damage done. This battle has been going on for nearly three hours. . . . It's no joke. It's a real war."[6]

By Sunday evening, reality set in. The fear of a second wave of attack gripped all Americans, especially those living on the West Coast. A day earlier the thought of a country 5,500 miles away attacking California was crazy. Not so on the evening of December 7. That night a Seattle radio station announced that there would be no regular radio programs broadcast that evening. Instead, the announcer gave instructions for how Americans might protect themselves and their cities.

Every person was to follow "blackout orders." Every house, from Mexico to Canada, must be curtained so lights could not signal an enemy plane overhead that people lived there. Ordinary window shades were not sufficient.

People must cover their windows with heavy drapes or black paper. Go outside, the announcer told the audience. Check to see that no light is escaping. Drivers must dim or shade the headlights on their cars and trucks. By eleven o'clock,

The USS *Shaw* explodes during the Japanese raid on Pearl Harbor, December 7, 1941.

INSIDE THE NEWSROOM: THE TELETYPE MACHINE

Most radio and newspaper newsrooms had a Teletype machine. A strip of white paper, called a "ticker," would print out news stories. The editor or writer on duty would periodically review the stories and decide which to print or broadcast.

When an important news story happened—termed "breaking news"—a bell on the Teletype machine would clang a number of times to alert the news staff that something critical was being transmitted.

In the New York newsroom of WOR Radio, on December 7, 1941, the bell rang at 2:25 p.m. The words that followed on the ticker tape were hard to believe: "White House says Japs attack Pearl Harbor."

all people must be in their homes. They must turn off all the lights. They could not use the telephones.

Americans listened, and they obeyed. Some people even went into the streets to scold drivers who had not blackened their headlights. That evening in Los Angeles, often called the "City of Lights," people stood outside in almost total blackness. Looking up, they saw the stars as they had not for a long time.

On Monday morning, workers began building sentry boxes, or guardhouses, at the entrances to the White House. Inside, the staff was equally busy. Some measured the long windows for heavy draperies that would become blackout curtains. Some distributed gas masks. In one office, engineers discussed building a bomb shelter under the nearby Treasury Building.

At 12:30 p.m. that day, President Roosevelt traveled from the White House to the Capitol. He wore a black band around his arm. It was a symbol of mourning for the more than one thousand people, primarily American soldiers, who had died at Pearl Harbor. In front of the president's podium was a fan of radio microphones. Each microphone had a label identifying the call letters of the radio networks: NBC for the National Broadcasting Company, CBS for the Columbia Broadcasting System, MBS for the Mutual Broadcasting System. These networks recorded the president's speech.

Hundreds of miles away in the streets of New York City, a large crowd of people gathered around a radio sound truck to listen to the president's speech. In homes, businesses, and schools, wherever there was a radio, people stood close and listened as the president asked Congress to declare war on Japan.

PRISONERS OF WAR IN THE
SOUTH PACIFIC

Shelley Smith was working in the research department of *Life* magazine when she met and fell in love with one of the magazine's photographers, Carl Mydans. In 1938, a woman usually quit her job once she married. *Life*'s editors, however, had different plans for Shelley. She had proven to be a good researcher and writer. Carl was one of their best photographers. Together, they could make a great news team. The magazine sent them first to Europe. Shelley hunted down background information on news events and people. She wrote captions for Carl's photographs and occasionally wrote longer articles. In 1940, *Life* sent them to China.

While Martha Gellhorn was reporting on the war in China for Collier's, Shelley and Carl were living in a mud hut in Chungking. In this mountainous area many Chinese had never seen a camera. They did not understand what a photograph was. Each day and often at night, Japanese planes bombed the city. Whenever the air-raid sirens began, the people took shelter in caves they had dug into the mountainside. The foreign journalists took cover there as well.

In October 1941, *Life* sent its roving reporters to the capital city of the Philippines in the South Pacific. Compared to the harsh conditions in Chungking, Manila was paradise. There were palm groves and fragrant plants—gardenias, frangipani, and orchids. The Mydanses rented a room in a hotel near the bay. On warm afternoons they could sit on the hotel's wide verandah under a slow-stirring ceiling fan and sip a glass of fresh-squeezed papaya juice.

Thousands of Americans lived in the Philippines. Some were soldiers. Some were civilians. Shelley spent her days researching stories. One story was about the sugar plantations in the hills. Another was about General Douglas MacArthur and the American soldiers stationed on the islands. Their mission was to defend the Philippine Islands alongside the Philippine army. The information Shelley had uncovered was troubling. The American forces lacked equipment, and the Filipino army had little training or experience in combat. Worse, the islands had few air-raid shelters. The city was hundreds of years old, and in some sections the streets were narrow and the houses made of wood. Bombs were deadly, of course. But the real threat to the lives of the people in the city was fire.

Still, for the time being, life was peaceful in the Philippines. Air raids did not scream during the night. No one hid in mountain caves. An American army nurse stationed in Manila wrote home to her mother in Indiana in November of that year, "Everything is quiet here so don't worry. You probably hear a lot of rumors, but that is all there is about it."[7]

On the morning of December 8, Carl Mydans rose early and reached for the newspaper. The headline shocked him. The Japanese had invaded Pearl Harbor. A few hours later planes with the rising sun painted red on the wings began bombing Manila. Carl grabbed his cameras, and he and Shelley ran into the streets.

One of the photographs Carl took was of American bomber pilots taking cover in a shallow trench. The Japanese had destroyed their planes on the ground. As on the airfield in Pearl Harbor, the fighter planes in Manila had been parked wingtip to wingtip. They were easy targets.

After the attack Shelley interviewed two American soldiers who had been on the ground at Clark Field. They had fired antiaircraft guns at the Japanese planes but with little effect. They admitted to the reporter that this was the first time they had ever shot at a live target. Shelley wrote the story for *Life*, quoting the two young men from Carlsbad, New Mexico. The first soldier, Sergeant Womack, had been writing a letter home when the attack began. He told Shelley, "All I got down was, 'Dear Mom,' and then . . . it happened. I put the letter in my pocket (I've still got it) and jumped up to the gun."[8]

Shelley asked the second soldier, Sergeant Smith, to describe the attack and his response. As the planes dove over him, he said, he "let out" with machine-gun fire. "They came so close we could have reached up and slapped them," he said. The planes were so close, in fact, that Sergeant Smith could see the helmets and goggles the pilots wore. All these details Shelley recorded and then wrote into her story for *Life*.

Carl and Shelley shipped their film and story to the magazine's editors in New York City on a commercial plane out of Manila. They had no way of knowing it would be the last plane to leave the capital—and the last story they would send—for a very long time. It took weeks for the story to arrive in New York City. On December 22, *Life* published Shelley's story with Carl's photographs, giving it the title "Defenders of Philippines."

By the time the story appeared in print, however, the situation in Manila was desperate. The planes of the rising sun had returned again and again. Fires burned daily. Black plumes of smoke rose in a dozen different locations around the city. Hospitals could not care for all the wounded. Drugstores ran out of bandages and medicines. Promises circulated—supplies were on the way, but each day no relief ship arrived. Worse, with such great naval losses at Pearl Harbor, no military ships would soon be coming to the rescue.

General MacArthur and his army retreated first to Bataan, then eventually to the island of Corregidor. Hundreds of American soldiers did not escape. The Japanese had drawn a net around Manila. And trapped inside were wounded soldiers and the nurses who cared for them. Trapped also were Carl and Shelley Mydans.

On New Year's Eve came an unexpected opportunity, one last chance to escape. Friends of the

Mydanses who were also foreign correspondents had learned of a freighter leaving Manila Bay for Corregidor before midnight. The friends made arrangements to board a tug that would take them to the ship. Shelley and Carl discussed what they should do. Within days, the Japanese would occupy the city. If they stayed, the Mydanses would be "enemy aliens." Quite likely, the Japanese would imprison them. On the other hand, the fighting continued on Corregidor. Although the Americans and Filipinos were fighting bravely, the Japanese were

Shelley and Carl Mydans smile for the cameras as they arrive safely home in America after more than two years in Japanese prisoner of war camps.

overpowering them. Escaping to Corregidor did not mean escaping to freedom. The Mydanses decided to stay.

Two days later the Japanese entered Manila. Shelley and Carl had only a few hours to gather what food and clothing they could carry in bundles. They boarded a truck with other Americans. The Japanese transported them to Santo Tomas University. High stone walls surrounded the old university, which had been built three hundred years earlier by missionaries to the islands. Now barbed wire topped the stone walls. The Japanese had turned the university into a prisoner of war camp.

Inside, thousands of men, women, and children lived "belly to back" on bamboo cots on the classroom floors. Food was often just boiled oats, wormy rice, or greasy fish soup, barely warm. Bedbugs were a menace. The prisoners formed a sanitation committee in an effort to keep their living quarters clean. As part of this committee, Shelley's job was to pick insects—weevils and beetles—out of the cereal. There was never enough food. Malnutrition weakened many. Mosquitoes carried diseases like malaria. The sick shivered on straw mats on the floor. Even for the healthy, the uncertainty of what the Japanese might do to them was maddening. The guards often slapped their prisoners. Worse were the rumors they

heard of brutality outside the prison walls: Japanese soldiers bayoneted the wounded American and Filipino soldiers. Shelley would later describe being a POW as living in "a constant, oozing fear."

When the Japanese discovered that Shelley and Carl worked for *Life*, they offered to release them. In exchange for their freedom, the correspondents must agree to work for the Japanese. To collaborate with the enemy was treason. The Mydanses refused.

Back in the United States the publisher of *Life* magazine waited anxiously to learn what had happened to his husband-and-wife team. Had they died during the bombings of Manila? Had they escaped the Japanese? If so, where in the South Pacific were they? Months passed. Finally, in November 1942, *Time* published hopeful news: Carl and Shelley Mydans were alive. They were prisoners of war.

A few weeks later, in its holiday issue, *Time* did not let its readers forget the price war correspondents were paying to cover the war. Carl and Shelley Mydans were beginning their second year as POWs. The magazine publisher wrote, "I hope the Japs know this is Christmas and give them a break." [9]

Eleven more months would pass before the readers of *Life* heard truly good news. In a prisoner exchange in 1943, Carl and Shelley Mydans had been released. The roving reporters returned to America

on a Swedish ship, the *Gripsholm*. They had lost weight, as all POWs had. Litter bearers carried the weakest off the ship on stretchers. Shelley and Carl, however, walked down the gangplank. One of the first things Shelley hoped to do now that she was back home in America was hunt down a hairdresser. After that she wanted to go back to work as a war correspondent.

These female workers on the home front are welding steel on a ship that will be named the SS *George Washington Carver*, after a famous African-American inventor and educator.

PAPER DOLLS ON THE
HOME FRONT

In America war changed everything. War separated families. Fathers and husbands, brothers and sons enlisted to fight. Women, too, enlisted, as nurses in the armed forces. They enlisted also in new military units created just for women. In 1942, the U.S. Congress established the Women's Army Auxiliary Corps, or WAAC. Soon after, the navy formed a women's corps called the WAVES (Women Accepted for Volunteer Emergency Service). Although women could not fight in combat, they could still serve. Women in these military units drew maps, operated radios and telephones, and studied and predicted the weather, which was essential for planning military maneuvers. They translated codes, repaired jeeps, flew planes, and even trained pigeons and dogs for war service.

War changed the way Americans lived. Families learned to recycle or do without items that the government needed in order to fight the war: gasoline, rubber, aluminum steel. Even grease, or fats from the frying pan, was saved and brought to recycling centers. The grease was used for making explosives. Women gave up silk stockings because silk was needed to make parachutes.

War changed the way Americans worked. Factories that once produced automobiles now began manufacturing airplanes. New factories opened to produce other necessary war materials: ships, tanks, jeeps, and ammunition. Thousands of men left their jobs to enlist in the military. Thousands of women took their places in the factories.

The same was true in newsrooms across the country. In 1942, *Time* reported that 173 men had left their jobs with the magazine in order to enlist in the military. Two "girls" had also resigned. One enlisted in the WAAC and the other in the WAVES. As thousands of men across the country left newsrooms to go to war, women filled the empty desks. Before the war the United Press had one newswoman on its staff, Ruby Black. During the war approximately sixty-five women worked for the UP. The same was true for other news organizations. The women wrote hard news as well as soft. They attended press conferences, sat in the galleries of the Senate and Congress to report

VICTORY WAITS ON _YOUR_ FINGERS—

KEEP 'EM FLYING, MISS U.S.A.

UNCLE SAM NEEDS STENOGRAPHERS! ✦ GET CIVIL SERVICE INFORMATION AT YOUR LOCAL POST OFFICE

U.S. CIVIL SERVICE COMMISSION, WASHINGTON, D.C.

The Royal Typewriter Company produced this poster, encouraging women to apply for government jobs during the war. Women were needed to take the place of men who had enlisted or were drafted to fight in the war.

on the workings of the government. They covered fires and bank robberies and other police business. And they still wrote the women's page. News was in demand! Americans simply couldn't get enough information, not only about the war but also about the efforts to win the war on the home front. The number of people buying newspapers and magazines soared.

War may have opened doors for women reporters, but prejudice remained. The press called them "paper dolls." It was not a compliment. During the Great Depression paper dolls became a popular children's toy. The flat figures cut from cardboard were flimsy. The cardboard bends; the paper rips. To call women reporters paper dolls was to suggest they lacked sturdiness and substance.

At least two male reporters, Stanley Frank and Paul Sann, expressed real surprise that the newspapers all across the country hadn't turned into tabloids of gossip and rumors and recipes once the women entered the newsrooms. In a magazine article these two men wrote:

> Paper dolls are reading copy, working on the rewrite desk, taking pictures. They are covering riots, crimes of purple passion, train wrecks, fires and suicides without swooning. Much to the astonishment of [many] . . . the paper always appears on time, it is reasonably free of errors and there has not yet been a deluge of libel suits or indignant readers canceling their subscriptions. [10]

Walter Bodin, city editor of the *Oakland Tribune* in California, wasn't as favorable about the paper dolls on his staff. He said:

> No matter how able they are, all are given to chattering among themselves. They are coy and warm by turns; they clutter and clatter endlessly. Every afternoon, just after the home-edition deadline, the local room presents the sight and sound of a meeting of neurotic clubwomen. The atmosphere demoralizes the men. I have to restrain myself violently from . . . serving tea and ladyfingers at three o'clock. But all I can do is hum "God Bless America" . . . and pray fervently for the end of this war. [11]

For the time being, however, someone had to research, write, and print the news. Women welcomed the chance. One of those women knocking on the newsroom door in 1942 was Marguerite Higgins.

For Marguerite, the journey to war began when she was a child. She listened to her father's tales of driving an ambulance in the First World War. As she grew older, Marguerite read war novels. The "agonized descriptions" were unlike anything her father had told her. War novels were "all pain and futile death." Nevertheless, the war stories left their mark. If there was ever war during her lifetime, she wanted to be a part of it—if not as a soldier, then as a war correspondent.

Marguerite Higgins was twenty-one years old and had just graduated from college when America declared war on Japan. She had traveled to New York City hoping to get a job as a news reporter. Like Frances Lide, Marguerite's first efforts failed. By the time she entered the offices of the *New York Herald Tribune*, Marguerite understood she'd never land a job unless she could first get past the receptionist. This time she squared her shoulders and simply walked briskly past the reception-ist's desk as if she were one of the staff going to her desk. Her ploy worked. Inside the city newsroom, however, she stopped and stared. "I had never seen so many typewriters all in one place, or been in such a relentlessly brightly lit room," she said. Her confidence slipped, but only for a moment. She had gotten herself this far. She wasn't going to turn back.

The city editor was L. L. Engelking. In the 1930s, one of his best front-page writers had been Ishbel Ross. The fact that Marguerite was a woman wasn't the problem. Her young age and inexperience were. Still, he offered her the slimmest hope. "Maybe later," he said.

Marguerite stayed in New York City and enrolled in graduate school to study journalism. Months later she got a tip. The *Herald Tribune* had an opening for a newswriter on the city desk. Marguerite wasted no time. She knocked again on L. L. Engelking's door.

Clearly, Marguerite was intelli-gent and aggressive. "You think you can do it, eh?" the editor asked.

People all across America had been asking women this same ques-tion since the war had begun. Do you think you can work in a factory assembling grenades and bombs? Do you think you can build a ship? Can you drive a bus, fly a plane, type one hundred words a minute? The women had answered, "Yes." So did Marguerite. "I *know* I could do a good job for you," Marguerite told the editor. [12]

L. L. Engelking gave in. He asked her to start that day.

Marguerite Higgins was not a paper doll. She did not chatter or nibble cupcakes after writing her stories, and she didn't know any women reporters who did. Still, she was smart enough to realize the odds were against her. Besides being young and inexperienced, she had other disadvantages: She was blond and she was beautiful. "Some male officials associate the combination of femininity and blond hair with either dumbness or slyness or both," she said. [13] Marguerite Higgins was deter-mined to prove them wrong. War or no war, she was going to earn her byline and make a name for herself in this business.

ENEMY ALIENS
IN AMERICA

Decca Records had released a new song. The lyrics were upbeat and confident.

> We did it before and we can
>   do it again;
> And we'll do it again . . .
> We're one for all and all for
>   one.

The song was a big hit, but the lyrics weren't exactly true. Yes, Americans had "done it before." They had defeated the enemy in the last world war. But in some western states, California in particular, the country was not united "all for one." Some Americans turned against others, particularly those of Japanese heritage.

> We'll knock them over and
>   then
> We'll get the guy behind
>   them.

"Them" were the Japanese. Many Americans did not see a difference between the Japanese ruled by Emperor Hirohito and those who had immigrated to the United States many years earlier to become peaceful and productive American citizens. To some Americans, all Japanese, even those who had been born in this country, were the enemy. Each day Americans read grim headlines about the war in the South Pacific. The island of Guam had fallen almost immediately to Japanese forces. By March 1942, the Japanese had defeated American troops in Manila, Bataan, and Corregidor. More than thirty-six thousand American men and women were now prisoners of war. General MacArthur had retreated to Australia.

Despite the hit songs on the radio, the United States Navy had lost more than eighty ships and thousands of soldiers. On the home front the American people responded with fear and frustration, anger and anxiety. The word "Jap" was a slur used by news reporters and politicians. It appeared on war posters promoting patriotism. "Jap" became part of everyday conversations, spoken with bitterness, suspicion, and ill will. Some Japanese Americans put signs in their store windows: I AM AN AMERICAN. The signs made little difference.

Racist attitudes were evident

Dorothea Lange took this photograph of Japanese-American children pledging allegiance to the American flag. Days later, the children and their families were transported to internment camps.

Many Thanks for your Patronage. Hope to Serve you in Near future. God be with you till w a. meet again.

Mr. and Mrs. K. Iseri

Mr. and Mrs. Iseri put this sign in their drugstore window, thanking all their customers who had supported them over the years. As Japanese Americans, the Iseri family had to give up their business and relocate to an internment camp for the duration of the war.

elsewhere—in political cartoons published in newspapers and magazines, on signs posted in neighborhoods. And on billboards. America was not only at war with the country of Japan. America was also at war, it seemed, with the Japanese race. Americans wrote letters to newspapers expressing their distrust, even their hatred, of these people. "It's a question of whether the white man lives on the Pacific Coast or the brown men. They came into this valley to work, and they stayed to take over," said Austin Anson, a farmer in California. [14]

The man in charge of defending the homeland on the Pacific coast was Lieutenant General John L. DeWitt. He trusted no one of Japanese ancestry, no matter where they had lived or worked or gone to school. He wanted all Japanese on American soil imprisoned. Only then, he said, could the home front be safe. He testified before Congress: "A Jap's a Jap. It makes no difference whether he is an American citizen or not. I don't want any of them. . . . They are a dangerous element, whether loyal or not." [15]

On February 19, 1942, the president signed Executive Order 9066. All Japanese Americans had to give up their property and move to government-run camps. These Japanese Americans were not spies. They were not collaborating with the enemy, nor were they accused or found guilty of committing a crime.

They were, however, considered "enemy aliens."

An alien is someone who lives in American but is not an American citizen. During World War II, enemy aliens were people the government considered a threat to the country. Five classes of people were labeled "enemy aliens" during World War II: any person suspected of espionage; Germans; Italians; Japanese; and finally, all American-born Japanese.

The government restricted what the Japanese Americans could take with them to the camps: clothing, bedding, and eating utensils. Automobiles and household furniture and appliances must be left behind. Family pets were forbidden in the camps and must also be given away. The Japanese Americans had only a few weeks to sell everything they owned or somehow find a way to store their goods during their absence. No one knew how long the war might last, but as long as the fighting continued, so too would the imprisonment of these enemy aliens.

Almost ten years earlier Dorothea Lange had stood at her studio window and watched a man in the street below unsure of where he should go. She had taken her camera and ventured into the streets of San Francisco to photograph the hungry and the homeless. Throughout the 1930s, she had continued to work on occasion for the government. She was not a "star photographer" the way Margaret Bourke-White was. Dorothea's photographs were not published on the cover of *Life* magazine. Even so, her type of documentary work during the Great Depression was exactly what the government wanted now. Dorothea accepted the job of photographing the relocation of Japanese Americans, but not because she believed what the government was doing was right. She felt an obligation to the Japanese Americans themselves. She did not understand the racism sweeping the country. How had this happened? she asked herself and others. How could a democracy treat its own citizens this way? Her photographs could make Americans aware of their racism.

Throughout the months of April and May 1942, Dorothea walked through the streets of San Francisco again. She went first to a section of the city called "Little Toyko," because this was where many people of Japanese ancestry lived. Most had lived here all their lives. Many had been born here.

On Post Street she saw a man and his son in overalls, boarding up the front of their optometry shop. She wandered through the neighborhoods, photographing teenagers sitting on porch steps. One teenage boy wore a letter sweater from his high school, given to him for his athletic achievements. She went to the Raphael Weill School, where

Living conditions in the internment camps were grim. Dorothea Lange took this photograph of a dust storm at Manzanar, California.

elementary-age children pledged alliance to the flag. Were these children America's enemies? she asked.

Weeks passed. The city of San Francisco began to change. The section of the city known as "Japantown" was empty. TO LEASE signs hung in windows of empty storefronts. Restaurants were empty. The streets were empty.

Early on the morning of May 20, 1942, Dorothea returned to the Raphael Weill School, where a few weeks earlier she had photographed smiling children. Now six Greyhound buses waited. Armed military police lined the streets, but there was no need for rifles. Bundled in coats and carrying what they could, the families filed peacefully onto the buses. Each person, adults as well as children, wore a paper tag tied to his or her clothing. The label identified who they were. A newspaper reporter, quite possibly a "paper doll," described the scene for the *San Francisco Chronicle*:

There were tears—but
not from the Japanese.
They came from those
who stayed behind—old
friends, old employers, old
neighbors. By noon, all
274 people were at
Tanforan, registered,
assigned to their
temporary new homes
and sitting down to lunch.

The Japanese were gone
from San Francisco. [16]

Where had they gone? No state in the Union wanted them. And so the government set up camps at racetracks and on fairgrounds. In all, 110,000 men, women, and children became inmates of the government-run camps. Barbed wire surrounded these camps, too. Armed soldiers manned the sentry posts to ensure no one escaped. Dorothea took her camera inside the camps. She photographed the tar-paper-covered barracks. Families shared single rooms. In some instances, the "room" was a horse stall swept out and set up with narrow beds and thin mattresses. Most housing units had no running water or cooking facilities. People stood around with nothing to do. Some teenagers played baseball. Some men carved little animals from scraps of wood. Children, in particular, did not understand what was happening. "I wonder who found this desert and why they put us in a place like this," asked one child.

To force innocent people to give up their comfortable homes and ways of earning a living and to place them under armed guards in crowded, shabby barracks was shameful, Dorothea said. "What was of course horrifying," she added, "was to do this thing completely on the basis of what blood may be coursing through a person's veins, nothing else."[17]

She did not express her horror in the captions she wrote for her photographs. Rather, she wrote simply and without emotion as the government had instructed her. The images, however, suggested much more than words could say. "A hot windstorm brings dust from the surrounding desert," she captioned one photograph. The picture showed an American flag flying at the Manzanar camp. The long row of buildings on either side disappear in the dust.

During the Depression, when Dorothea had photographed the migrant workers, she believed she was helping them. They had taught her courage, and she had captured that courage on film. Now, once more, she believed her photographs could somehow help the Japanese-American people as well. In these photographs, too, Dorothea captured their courage and dignity.

"You put your camera around your neck along with putting on your shoes, and there it is, an appendage of the body that shares your life with you," she said. "The camera is an instrument that teaches people how to see without a camera."[18]

What did Dorothea want the people to see? Injustice, suffering, indignity—these were the images she captured.

The term "concentration camp" sent chills through Americans.

Newspapers had hinted at such camps in Germany and Poland, where terrible tortures were happening to the people imprisoned there. Americans seethed with anger knowing their soldiers and even their nurses and war correspondents were in Japanese POW camps. Why, then, did Americans allow internment camps in their own country, imprisoning their own citizens?

Perhaps one reason is that the general public did not see the injustices of Executive Order 9066. Dorothea's photographs of the crude barracks and the boredom behind barbed wire were not front-page news. They became the property of the U.S. government. For each photograph she took, Dorothea had to submit its negative also. She could not make copies to tack on her studio wall or to distribute to others.

Dorothea's photographs remained unseen for many years, locked away in government files. Still, her work was very important. Her photographs were a vivid record of racism in America during a time of great fear and uncertainty.

> **The correspondents who were going with the troops were down in the south. They were sent down there well ahead of time. So the rest of us had no idea—we didn't know until it happened—the morning of June 6. Well, we heard planes, you know, just hordes of planes—the sky was black with them. I don't know, it was probably about five in the morning.**

★HELEN KIRKPATRICK

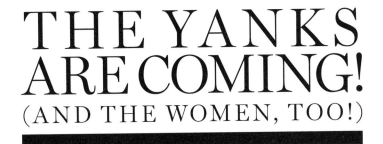

Chapter Five

THE YANKS ARE COMING!
(AND THE WOMEN, TOO!)

On the day the Japanese bombed Pearl Harbor, the people of England were as surprised as the Americans. And yet hopes soared. America's declaration of war meant England was no longer alone in the fight against Hitler.

Seven weeks after Pearl Harbor, Helen Kirkpatrick stood once again on the docks—this time in Belfast, Ireland. She wore a military-like uniform. A patch with a large letter *C* on the sleeve indicated that she was now a war correspondent. In the harbor that winter morning were two American transport ships. The passengers had begun marching down the gangplanks. They were the first American troops to arrive in the British Isles. With them were American army nurses. The Britons called the Americans "Yanks."

Helen's news coverage that day described the excitement in the air. A military band played "The Star-Spangled Banner." Crowds cheered. Dressed in heavy overcoats and helmets, the troops marched in formation from the wharf through the streets of Belfast. Each carried a rifle at one shoulder and a pack slung over the other. Irish children marched alongside them, laughing. The Yanks were coming!

The Yanks would continue to come. Over the next few months additional transport ships brought doctors, nurses, and Red Cross recreation workers, as well as troops and much-needed supplies and weaponry: planes, jeeps, tanks. The Yanks had not come to rescue England. They had come to fight alongside the British as an ally. Now American bombers—B24

Liberators—lifted off from British airfields into the sky like great dark birds. They flew across the English Channel on bombing raids over Belgium and Germany.

Other allies were mustering in England as well, including soldiers from Canada, France, and Poland. Preparations had begun for a massive land invasion of France, though no one knew when or where that invasion would happen.

Thousands of miles away the Yanks and their allies had landed in North Africa. They defeated the German Nazis in the desert. They pushed across the Mediterranean Sea and defeated the Italian Fascists in Sicily. They pushed forward again, into mainland Italy. The war correspondents pushed forward with them. War news not only kept the people back home informed. It boosted morale, so it could help to win the war.

The free world was fighting back, and the women war correspondents would play a key role in the battles yet to come. One of those women was Toni Frissell.

General Patton talks to a U.S. soldier near Sicily, Italy, in 1943.

BLACKOUTS, BARRAGE BALLOONS, AND THE AMERICAN RED CROSS

In the last two hours of Toni Frissell's flight across the Atlantic Ocean, the pilot turned off all the lights in the cabin. Even airplanes followed blackout rules during wartime. The passengers who had boarded in New York City included fashion photographer Toni Frissell.

Before the war Toni's work had appeared in two popular women's magazines, *Vogue* and *Harper's Bazaar*. On this flight across the Atlantic, she was not representing those magazines. She was not a photojournalist in the same way as Dorothea Lange or Margaret Bourke-White was. Still, she was certain her skills as a photographer could help the war effort. And so she had volunteered for an assignment for the American Red Cross.

The mission of the Red Cross was to boost the morale of the American soldiers wherever they might be shipped—North Africa, Italy, England. Toni's mission was to document the good work being done by the Red Cross so that people back home, when they saw her pictures, would continue to support the organization.

When the plane landed in England, Toni stepped out into bright sunshine. One of the first things she noticed was "dozens of silver barrage balloons," sailing in and out of the clouds. This balloon curtain was one of England's defenses against the bombing raids during the Blitz. Cables hung from each sixty-foot-long hydrogen-filled balloon. The cables could shear off the wing of an airplane. To avoid the cables, German pilots had to fly above the balloons. The higher altitude made bombing their targets more difficult. Pilots who risked flying low came within the range of antiaircraft guns on the ground, which the British called "ack-acks" for the sound the guns made. Thousands of balloons floated over England. Toni joked, "It looked as though England were being held up by blimps."[1]

Toni's assignment took her to U.S. Army hospitals. Lying in the hospital cots were the wounded who had been transported to England from Italy, where American troops were fighting hard against Mussolini's army. The Red

Wherever the soldiers went, the American Red Cross was not far behind. In Assam, India, in 1944, these Red Cross workers helped soldiers enjoy a few hours of R&R-rest and relaxation.

Cross recreation girls who lived at the hospital moved among the cots, chatting with the wounded soldiers and writing letters for those who could not manage to hold a pen. Toni, too, moved among the cots, taking photographs.

The Red Cross set up recreation centers. Stepping inside one was a little bit like going home. American music played on the radio. Visitors could shoot darts, play cards, or just drink a hot cup of coffee and talk with a real American girl. In one photograph Toni captured a group of soldiers and Red Cross girls dancing in a conga line. Even during the war, people found ways to laugh and enjoy one another.

Toni's mission also took her into field camps where medical teams were preparing for the Allied invasion of France. She walked the streets of London, taking photographs of a city that had suffered from months of bombing. Toni photographed St. Paul's Cathedral. All the buildings around the church had been destroyed during the Blitz, but the cathedral stood untouched in the midst of the ruins. Toni described one neighborhood as "a valley of destruction." She looked up at a brick building. She could see right into the bedroom. The exterior wall was gone, and a white iron bed hung on the edge, about to crash to the street. "The torn sheets were fluttering in the wind," Toni said.

She walked on. When she turned the corner, she stopped cold. "A small boy was sitting at the bottom of a high pile of haphazard planks and beams. I was told he had come home from playing and found his house in shambles—his mother, father and brother dead under the rubble."

His coat was too large for him. His socks had fallen and bunched around his ankles. He was not crying. "He was looking up at the sky," Toni said, "his face an expression of both confusion and defiance." [2]

Toni stepped closer and took his photograph.

"The worst part of war, in my opinion," said Toni, "is what happens to the survivors—the widows without home or family, the ragged kids left to wander." [3]

Toni had come to England on an assignment for the American Red Cross. Her assignment was not the war front. Even so, she had discovered a corner of the war behind the front lines that was just as tragic. "The after effects of war are never pretty to see," she said. "Neither should they be forgotten."

Her photographs made certain they would not be.

Toni Frissell first photographed the war in England for the Red Cross. Note the Red Cross pin on her blouse and the Red Cross patch on her sleeve.

"CHILDREN
ARE SOLDIERS, TOO"

In 1943, Martha Gellhorn was still another Yank to land on British soil. She, too, now wore the military uniform and the armband of a war correspondent. Her work in Spain and in China, in addition to the book she had published about the Great Depression, had earned her quite a reputation as a writer. *Time* magazine had called her one of *Collier's* "star reporters." The sort of stories she wrote best were not about admirals and generals. Instead, she hunted for—and always found—stories about ordinary people and their strength of character.

One of her first stories was called "The Price of Fire." It was about a burn center and the recuperation of the pilots who, in her words, "had crashed in planes or were thrown clear or dragged from the burning wreckage—but not quite soon enough."[4] She wrote about their scars and their pain in a sensitive way, without exaggeration or melodrama the way a "sob sister" might have done ten years earlier.

One night Martha set out to discover how war had changed England's teenagers. A group of boys and girls led her through the narrow streets in London's East End. Because of the blackout, the night was dark as pitch. A flashlight would help, but batteries were hard to get and cost too much.

They took her to their hangout, a club on Mulready Road. The place had just three bare, colorless rooms. Some boys were playing table tennis. Others had removed their shoes and shirts to exercise. Martha noticed that their socks and undershirts were gray. Soap, too, was costly during wartime. Upstairs, a group of girls drank cocoa and gossiped about boys. When they learned Martha was a Yank, they asked excitedly, "Have you ever met Humphrey Bogart?" He was their favorite movie star, they told her.

Their laughter surprised Martha. German bombs had gutted their houses. They no longer went to school. During the day they worked in factories and war industries. At night, if they had a little extra money, they went to the picture shows, where American movies played. "They are anything but sad," Martha would later write. "They

are the liveliest, toughest, brightest people you could ever hope to meet."

She called them her friends. They had no idea why the Yank wanted to write a story about them. She asked them what difference the war had made in their lives. Not much, really, answered a young man named Ben. He worked as a plumber. "We're working class people and we never did eat so much as all that, and it's about as good now as it ever was."

What do you want for yourself once the war ends? Martha asked the group.

One wanted to go back to school. Another wanted a better house for his family. Then a shy young man spoke up. "I want a greyhound to race at White City." [5]

The friends exploded in laughter. In their eyes, his dream was so fantastic, so impossible to achieve, it was as if he had told a grand joke.

Someone played a few records, and the friends jitterbugged. They had learned the popular dance, they said, "by watching it in American movies." By 10:30 p.m., they had shut off the record player and left the club. Their workday tomorrow began at 6:00 a.m.

Their story, too, was a war story. Later, alone at her typewriter, Martha Gellhorn would write about these "poor kids of London." Most had worked since they were fourteen, she wrote. Each one contributed to the welfare of his or her family. They did so without complaining, because the right thing to do was to take care of one another. They were modest, these kids of London. They didn't think of themselves as really making much of a difference in the war, but they did, Martha insisted.

In America, *Collier's* published the story under the title "Children Are Soldiers, Too." Probably none of Martha's friends on Mulready Road read it. If they had, the title might have puzzled them. They did not think of themselves as children. And they certainly weren't soldiers. They were simply doing what had to be done.

As for her readers back in America, Martha had no way of knowing what they thought. Nor did she much care. She wrote for herself. She wrote, also, so that her readers might understand the many different ways war disrupts lives. When one story ended, she sent it off and turned her attention to the next story waiting to be found.

In London's East End, children sit outside their demolished homes.

RUMORS OF HOLOCAUST

Information from Nazi-occupied Europe continued to reach the free world. In England, Tania Long had reported on the newspapers of the underground resistance groups. Refugees who had escaped to England were another source of information. In her hunt for stories, Martha Gellhorn met and interviewed three Polish refugees.

"I tried to write most often of what was brave and decent," Martha said. These three men of different ages did not know one another. Each was brave and decent. And yet the stories they told her were horrific.

The first man had been a farmer before the war. After the occupation he became a farm slave and depended on his German owner for food and clothes. He was forty years old, Martha guessed. But he was thin and ill and could have been younger. He told Martha, "If a man shelters a Jew, the Germans shoot him and his whole family; they published an order that any Pole who gave a piece of bread to a Jew would be killed. We used to leave bread or whatever we had in the forests, where the Jews were hiding."[6]

The second man had been a university student before the war. The Gestapo captured him and sent him to a forced labor camp, but he jumped off the train and escaped. With the help of underground partisans, he changed his identity and became a bookkeeper in a German barrel factory. He secretly worked for the underground. He had watched as Nazis herded Jewish men, women, and children into the train yard and then onto cattle cars. He told Martha, "They were packed 130 to a cattle car, there were 46 carloads of them." He could hear their screams. He saw the cattle car sway with their efforts to free themselves. He'd had nightmares for weeks.[7]

The third refugee was also Polish, but unlike the others, he was Jewish. Before the war he had been a lawyer. During the war he lived in the ghetto in Warsaw. He told Martha, "The Germans built a wall ten feet high and sealed off this corner of the city. . . . As no one can grow food from cobblestones they were kept alive by the rations the Germans allowed them." Often, he said, the Nazis organized "shooting parties" and wandered through the ghetto taking shots. The people fled "like hunted animals."[8]

Martha felt only hatred for the Nazis. She could do nothing to help or change the situation in Poland. The only power she had was to write. Once again Martha sat at her typewriter. She titled this story simply, "Three Poles." She began with the line: "'In my village,' the man said, 'the people stood in front of the church and cried. . . .'"

Martha was not the first to write about Nazi atrocities. Newspapers had printed numerous stories of forced labor, starvation, and death camps. But a writer does not choose a story because no one else has told it before. She selects a story because it must be told, because it is important, and because in the telling, some good may come from it. Martha wrote "Three Poles" for those reasons.

Kathryn Cravens, photographed here with General Eisenhower (*right*), began her career as an actress on radio programs during the 1930s. By 1945, she was among the few women radio news broadcasters and the only accredited female radio correspondent.

She wrote in her distinctive style—with her brand of language, vivid details, and passion.

She ended the story with hope. Germany had tried to turn Poland into "a cemetery," she wrote. But in Poland there were many thousands of men just like these "three Poles," who had resisted the Nazis and were resisting still. "The Germans have never been able to stop them," she wrote. [9]

The Yanks were coming. "And the Germans," Martha concluded, "who have ruled Poland and never conquered it must now be afraid."

The Yanks were coming, she told her readers. But she warned them too. They might not get there in time.

WHAT IS ACCREDITATION?

Although thousands of women now had jobs in newsrooms across the country, only a handful of women got the chance to go to war. Those who did were all experienced writers or photographers. Some, like Helen Kirkpatrick and Margaret Bourke-White, were already employed by a news organization. Others, like Martha Gellhorn, scrambled to find a publication that would hire them as a war correspondent. Martha called her old editor at *Collier's*.

No journalist, male or female, just hopped on an airplane or a ship and went to war. First, the journalist needed two important documents: a press pass signed by the War Department and a U.S. passport. Only reporters employed by news organizations or publications could receive a press pass. Martha Gellhorn had written some powerful stories about war in Spain and in China. But unless *Collier's* formally took her on, she had little chance of getting her press credentials.

Next, journalists had to sign an agreement. They would submit all copy for military review. In this way, the military could censor information that might give an advantage to the enemy. Censors removed any reference to the location of troops, ships, aircraft, or supplies. Even details about the weather in a city could tip the enemy to troop movements. The journalists also agreed to obey the orders of the military officers to whom they were assigned. Failure to do so could mean losing their valuable credentials.

Called "accreditation," this system determined who reported the war and how. It was much the same as it had been during the First World War. One thing was different, however. This time around, 127 of the war correspondents were women.

In the summer of 1943, *Collier's* notified Martha that she had received her accreditation. She said she was as happy as "a fire horse." Within weeks, she was headed for England.

PLANS FOR INVA$

By 1944, more than one hundred women had earned their accreditation from the War Department. And yet, even in war, they still faced the same prejudice that had dogged them during peacetime. Military officers often denied women assignments that would take them to the front where the fighting was. The women were "skirted" from military briefings. British General Montgomery, called "Monty," thought women on the battlefield were bad luck.

In the first years of the war, women often had to settle for writing stories with a woman's angle. As such, explained war correspondent Ruth Cowan, they covered the nurses or the field hospitals or the food served to the troops, not the fighting or the battles. Despite the restrictions, women journalists still found ways to get as close to the front lines as possible.

Helen Kirkpatrick, for example, managed to get assignments that took her close to the front in both Africa and Italy. In Italy she covered a field hospital that was considered a "forward unit." The Germans were "just over the hill," she said. She stayed for four days. "I helped in the operating room because they were terribly short-handed," she said. "They worked around the

clock practically, and errands I could do."

She received a m Colonel Frank Knox wanted to meet with her. The colonel's headquarters were behind the lines, in an Italian villa. Mud coated Helen's clothes. She managed somehow to find a clean uniform. The colonel told her he wanted her to return to England. Was he sending her back because she was a woman? she wondered. "You want me out of Italy?" she asked bluntly.

"No," he answered. Then he added, "But I think there are things that you ought to be doing in London."

Just what those "things" were Helen found out later. The Allies— led by American General Dwight Eisenhower, working closely with British General Montgomery and French General de Gaulle—were planning a massive invasion of Europe. The military command was preparing for an important news briefing. Hundreds of war correspondents were in England, but surely not all could attend the meeting. And so the military created "press pools," where one journalist represented a larger group of correspondents. The idea was that the correspondent invited to the briefing would then share the information with all the others within the pool. The military leaders asked Helen Kirkpatrick to represent the print pool, the group of reporters working for newspapers. Radio broadcaster Edward R. Murrow represented radio networks. Two other correspondents represented the magazines and the wire services. The subject of the top secret briefing was the Allied invasion of France. Of all the war correspondents in England, Helen was the only woman to attend the briefings.

"We met about once a week with the military," Helen said. "We covered how many people would go on the first wave of the invasion, how to get copy back to the press headquarters, where copy would be sent—either back to England or directly to the United States. All those practical kinds of questions."[10]

The invasion would happen both by air and by sea. Helen applied to accompany those soldiers crossing the English Channel into France by glider. The military placed her name on a list of correspondents who volunteered to accompany the invasion. Although the military had treated her equally during the months of briefings, they stopped short of sending her into combat. Someone, she never learned who for certain, removed her name from the list. The War Department assigned twenty-eight correspondents to cover the D-day invasion. All twenty-eight were men. Women

had earned their accreditation, but no woman would be allowed to witness the invasion firsthand. Women like Helen Kirkpatrick had earned the respect of the military command, but they were not yet on equal footing with men.

Allied troops wade "into the jaws of death" on the coast of Normandy during the D-day invasion. This photograph was taken by a male war correspondent because women correspondents were not allowed to accompany the troops on such a dangerous mission.

"THE FIRST HOSPITAL SHIP"

Before dawn on June 6, Helen Kirkpatrick heard the airplanes. She knew then that the D-day invasion had begun. If the invasion succeeded, then additional correspondents would cross the English Channel, perhaps in just a few days, to cover the action. Martha Gellhorn, however, could not wait. That night she made her way to the waterfront. At the docks was a hospital ship. Painted on the ship's white hull was a large red cross.

Military police stopped her from going farther. She showed them her papers indicating that she was an accredited war correspondent. She was going to interview the nurses aboard the hospital ship, she fibbed. The MPs let her through. Once aboard, Martha hid in a bathroom. She cowered there, sweating. She was "badly spooked," she said. If found out, the military would take away her accreditation. They might even arrest her or send her back to America. Still, to witness this great invasion was worth the risk.

Suddenly, the ship engines rumbled. She heard clacks and wrenching as the anchor was raised. The hospital ship was under way. Still, she waited a while longer. Then she unlocked the bathroom door and stepped out.

As the ship steamed toward the coast of France, Martha wandered below deck. She observed everything and took notes:

> 6 nurses aboard;
> 422 beds covered with
>   new blankets;
> bright, clean, well-
>   equipped operating
>   room;
> cans marked "Whole
>   Blood";
> plasma bottles, supplies
>   of drugs, bales of
>   bandages. [11]

Crossing the English Channel would take hours. The waiting was hard. Martha chatted with a nurse from Texas who passed the uneasy time by painting her fingernails a bright red. "I'm glad to be going just where I'm going," she told Martha. "Don't you know how happy those little old boys are going to be when they see us coming?"

Above the sound of the ship's engines, Martha could hear the drone of planes. They, too, were crossing into battle. As the ship neared the coast of France, the concussion of bombs jarred the ship. Martha climbed on deck. What she saw amazed her. Barrage balloons clouded the sky. Guns flashed a terrible lightning. The ship was so close to the shore that she could see troops unloading from ships to barges. On

RUTH COWAN REPORTS FROM LONDON

When Martha Gellhorn returned from her stowaway mission aboard the hospital ship, Ruth Cowan was among the correspondents waiting on the docks. On June 9, 1944, Ruth broadcast a story about the wounded returning from battle. Ruth's broadcast was most unusual simply because the radio broadcasters were mainly male. An excerpt from that broadcast follows:

I was on the dock when the first ships came in on the afternoon of D-day, bringing back the first American wounded. . . . There was no cheering when these ships came in. It was too serious. All of those on the dock had seen the ship loading. We had heard soldiers call out to one another, "Good luck, pal. See you later."

The walking wounded and those who can stand . . . are sent to hospitals inland by ambulances. . . . One man called out cheerfully, "We made it." Then the litter bearers went aboard. As they came down the gangplank carrying litters, they walked with a smooth, catlike tread to save the wounded soldiers an unnecessary jar. Those needing immediate care, the emergency operation cases, are sent to a field hospital, such as the one at which I am staying. High praise is due the Negro litter bearers. . . .

I was in an operating tent in the field hospital one night. . . . Some of the most skillful medical hands in America are at work in these tents. Just before I left the hospital, I looked in on a ward tent. New patients had arrived. [I saw] one of the first German POWs taken in France. He had been badly hit in the chest. Next to him was an American pilot, asleep.

Everyone is working hard. Some nurses are on duty twelve hours. . . . But the chief nurse said, "That is what we came over for."[12]

the beach, tanks moved very slowly up a hillside.

And then, Martha wrote, "everything happened at once." Lightweight motor boats, called "water ambulances," were lowered from the ship's side into the water. "Take her in slow," voices shouted. "Look sharp!"

The water ambulances churned toward the beach. The stretcher bearers carried the wounded from the beaches to the ambulances. Some carried the wounded on their shoulders. Then the ambulances maneuvered in the rough sea back to the hospital ship anchored in deeper water. The stretcher bearers then raised the wounded above their heads to the men on deck.

Hours passed. On the shore the fighting continued. And the water ambulances never stopped coming and going. Martha managed somehow to get into one of the ambulances. The tide was changing, however. She had to wade to shore in waist-high water. Everyone felt the urgency to get as many wounded as possible off the beach before dark. Some had spent a full day and night already on the stretchers. Another night on the beach would cut their chances of survival.

The Germans had built bunkers into the hills above the shore. Big guns there fired on the ships in the harbor and at the troops on the beach. They had also buried mines, a type of spring-triggered bomb, along the beaches. In the growing darkness Martha saw long rows of tape that marked a path on which to walk. This path had been cleared of mines. A step on either side of the tape, however, could mean triggering an explosion.

The tide was still out, and the water ambulances could not get in. Martha sat on the beach alongside the wounded, and again the waiting was hard. It was dark now. Suddenly, at the far end of the beach, antiaircraft fire began. There were no foxholes to crawl into, and even if there were, what of the wounded? She could not leave them. She felt

"small and helpless," she said, as if she had stepped into "an enormous, insane nightmare."[13]

The tide inched closer. Then, at last, the water ambulances came ashore. Once aboard the hospital ship, Martha forgot her notebooks and helped the nurses and orderlies in whatever ways she could. Some men needed to be fed, for they had been two days without food. Most needed water. Others needed jackets removed or their boots cut away from water-swollen feet.

Belowdecks, the ward that just hours ago had been empty and spotlessly clean was now a "black hole" of pain. Martha described the scene in the article "The First Hospital Ship." The nurses had cut away the bloody clothing from the wounded and tossed it into piles in the corners. Bottles of blood for transfusions hung from cords. The wounded cried out in their sleep, or moaned. Those who could not sleep whispered to one another. There was no panic, Martha wrote. The wounded trusted the doctors and the nurses. No one doubted that they would return safely in a few hours to the shores of England.

When England came into view, it was greener than Martha had ever seen it. Her journey to the front was over. She was the first woman correspondent to land on the beaches during the D-day invasion. But she had achieved that distinction by disobeying military orders.

Soon after Martha filed her story with *Collier's*, the military police arrested her. They took her credentials, then transported her to a nurses' training camp outside London. When the troops moved inland off the beaches of Normandy, these American army nurses would follow and establish evacuation hospitals just behind the front lines. They were anxiously waiting for their turn to embark. When the nurses left, the military told Martha, then she could go too. [14]

But that could be days! she argued. News was happening every minute on the other side of the English Channel!

Within hours, she began to plot her escape. She wasn't in a jail cell. Still, she was isolated with no travel papers. Somehow she had to get to mainland Europe. A solution suddenly presented itself. When she learned of a British pilot who was flying to Italy, she convinced him to take her along. Quite likely, he didn't know of Martha's arrest. He knew only that she was a war correspondent and the invasion of Europe had begun. He agreed to let her hitch a ride.

"I followed the war wherever I could reach it," she said. "I had been sent to Europe to do my job, which was not to report the rear areas or the woman's angle." [15] The military called her escape out of England insubordination. Martha called it doing her job.

> " I won't be the first woman journalist in Paris–by any means–but I'll be the first dame photographer . . . unless someone parachutes in. "
>
> ★LEE MILLER, PHOTOJOURNALIST

Chapter Six

LIBERATION

Four days after D-day the first army nurses landed on the beachhead of Normandy. They rolled up their pant legs and waded ashore. Jeeps then transported them and their heavy packs inland. They pitched tents in a field and made ready their hospital.

That night a barrage of artillery hounded them. The nurses slept with their helmets on. In the morning the first casualties began to arrive. "For nine days we never stopped," nurse Ruth Hess wrote to her friend back home in Louisville, Kentucky. "We cared for 1500 patients." She described the types of wounds: gunshot, fractures, pierced lungs and kidneys, "everything imaginable," she wrote.[1]

And then the army nurses packed everything up and moved again, farther inland. As the troops advanced, so did they. Being close to the troops meant saving more lives.

A few weeks after the D-day invasion an airplane circled a field in France. Lee Miller stared from the plane window. The American photojournalist had once lived in France but had not seen the country or her friends there during the five long years of Nazi occupation. "As we flew into sight of France I swallowed hard on what were trying to be tears," she said.

She worked for *Vogue*, an upscale fashion magazine for women. Before the war the pages of *Vogue* showed beautiful women in beautiful clothing. Although the readers of *Vogue* were women, the editors understood that these women longed for news from the front lines. Lee Miller's assignment was to write about the Forty-fourth Evacuation Hospital in France. The magazine could continue to publish fashion photographs, but it would also publish Lee Miller's images of war.

123

TENT HOSPITAL IN FRANCE

As she jeeped from the airfield to the tent hospital, Lee Miller saw road signs like totem poles at the crossroads. The names painted on the signs were in English, not French. They were code names that American troops could understand: Missouri Charlie, Missouri Baker, Vermont Red....

The evacuation hospital was in the middle of a cow field. Before setting up the tents, men had chased the cows around the field to trigger whatever booby traps and mines had not yet been found and disconnected. This hospital was a city of tents. From the outside, they all looked the same: "Long, dark, greenish-brown . . . bearing on one top side an enormous circle enclosing the red cross."[2]

Lee moved among the hospital beds, stopping at times to talk with or photograph a patient. She took notes. One soldier was conscious while the doctors made a plaster case for his leg. When Lee raised her camera, the patient smoothed his hair in place. "The next boy," she wrote, "was on his side. [The surgeons] were probing for scattered shell splinters and wood fibers from the vicious, colored wooden bullets the Nazis are using in close fighting." This soldier, she happily noted, would be okay and back in England probably before she was.

That afternoon an officer asked if she wanted to advance to a "field hospital" just six miles from the front line. Lee didn't hesitate. "I grabbed a pocketful of bulbs and films and clambered into a command car," she said.

Every case was life and death in the field hospital, Lee would later write. These were the men so seriously wounded that they might not survive the six-mile drive back to the evacuation hospital. Everything here was in motion— fast paced and urgent. The blood supply was low. The doctors and nurses were exhausted. Lee had no way of knowing if the editors at *Vogue* would publish the photographs she was taking. She didn't stop to think of that until later. She simply went to work.

> I wandered from tent to tent at will. No one found it abnormal that I should be taking photographs, asking questions, helping myself to a mask at an entrance, climbing on to a bale of laundry. I didn't flash a bulb without some warning to the surgeon, but I needn't have bothered, as he never flinched, even for near gunfire. . . .

For an hour or so I watched lives and limbs being saved, by skill, devotion, and endurance. Grave faces and tired feet passed up and down the tent aisles. . . .

We drove slowly home caught up in a convoy of carriers returning empty to the front—meeting other convoys of men and equipment thundering by in long, even streams, lit only by the tiniest of "cat-eye" guide lamps. . . . It was night, my day was done. Not so for all these men and women and the pitiful victims of the pink gunfire on the horizon. [3]

That night back at the evacuation hospital in a bunk provided for her, Lee placed her helmet sideways on her head so that she'd be protected as she slept. Although it was July, the night was so cold, she ached. Through the night, the dusty ambulances continued to arrive, and a new shift of doctors and nurses operated in the surgical tent.

The next morning the sun shone brightly. Lee had seen and photographed plenty, but there was more to tell.

The ground mist was drying off, and a few nurses rolled up the sides of their wall-tents to lie in the sun, wearing their long-handle G.I. underwear. . . . A group came single-file between the tent-stakes loosening their surgical whites. They washed away the sweat from all-night duty, and fell on their cots, dead beat. One said, "Nice, isn't it . . . now I can yawn." They were remarkably pretty girls, all of them, now that the strain lines in their faces were slightly erased—lean, fit, and open-hearted. [4]

Lee departed as she had arrived, by plane. In London she began to write. The words came slowly. Writing, she discovered, was harder than photographing. "Every word I write is as difficult as 'tears wrung from stone,'" she told her editor, Audrey Withers. [5] Just as she could not alter the images, she could not sugarcoat the words. This is the reality of what was happening, she told her editor. Each victory reported in the newspapers and on the radio came at the price of limbs and lives.

After she submitted her story, Lee wondered if it was any good. It might be months before she saw an issue of the magazine. She had no way of knowing what photographs, if any, Audrey might use.

When Audrey saw the photographs and read the story Lee had

written, she said she felt as if she had been right there inside the tents with the doctors and nurses. She knew her readers would feel the same way too. The war was an important news story, and even fashion magazines like *Vogue* felt compelled to address it in their pages. *Vogue*'s readers weren't just women, they were also daughters, wives, and mothers of men fighting on the front. These women were eager for news. Yes, Audrey assured Lee in a letter to her. Her story and her photographs were very good.

Martha Gelhorn was determined to follow the war "wherever it could reach." She risked losing her accreditation by reporting close to the front lines, often traveling without a military escort or permission.

THE SIEGE OF SAINT-MALO

The enemy's guns went "whistle bang whistle bang whistle bang, and broke in the trees, the roofs, the street."[6] Lee Miller had gotten herself into a fix. She had linked up with the Eighty-third Division as it fought its way through the French countryside toward Paris.

The Germans were retreating. They had surrendered the seaside town of Saint-Malo. At least that is what the military said when it had okayed Lee Miller's request to enter the city and photograph it. She hitched a ride in a jeep, carrying only her cameras and a blanket roll. When she caught up with the troops on the outskirts of Saint-Malo, she discovered that the Germans had not surrendered after all. The Eighty-third was fighting door-to-door, in backyards and in alleys, rooting out Nazi soldiers and snipers in cellars and on roofs. In a citadel, an old fortress in the city, hundreds of Nazis had dug in to fight to the finish.

Lee should have turned around and gone back the way she had come. She was supposed to be following behind the troops, not advancing with them on the front lines. Lee Miller thought about it and decided to stay. "I was the only photographer for miles around and I now owned a private war," she said. "I waved goodbye to the pals who had given me a lift and tried to take stock of the situation. There was plenty of work to do as pictures, and plenty of ways to help."[7]

The next morning Lee Miller was pinned down in a narrow street while German gunfire "went whistle bang" over her head. She somehow managed to escape into the safety of a villa where French and American troops had headquarters while the siege blasted on.

From there, she hitched another ride in a jeep with a major. Wherever they were willing to take her, she was willing to go. Although her commanding officer would not approve, the men of the Eighty-third seemed not to mind. "Every place I went they were delighted to see me—mostly because I was an American woman, partly because I was a journalist and they wanted to be in the papers like everyone else," she said.

Days passed. The whistle bangs stopped and started, stopped then started again. Then the final assault began. American bombers came in waves, dropping two-hundred-pound bombs on the citadel. Lee Miller described the assault: "Bombs away—a sickly death rattle . . . smoke—belching, mushrooming and columning—towering up, black and white. Our house shuddered and stuff flew in the window—more bombs crashing, thundering, flashing—like Vesuvius—the smoke rolling away in a sloping trail." [8]

The Nazis surrendered, and the Americans moved that much closer to liberating the city of Paris. Lee Miller's commanding officer, however, did not look kindly on the war correspondent's presence on the front lines. He sent a patrol into Saint-Malo to find her. "I was dragged back to safety," she later wrote to her editor at *Vogue*. "I've been in the 'dog house.'"

But not for long. Once the military released her and returned her valuable credentials, Lee set out for Paris. If she was lucky, she'd be the first woman photographer to document the liberation of the city.

Helen Kirkpatrick *(left)*, Lee Miller *(center)*, and Tania Long *(right)* pose in their correspondents uniforms in 1943.

PARIS IS FREE!

Helen Kirkpatrick also had hopes of being among the first correspondents to enter Paris with the Allied troops. Wearing pants, combat boots, and a helmet, she rode along with the troops in a military jeep. In camp at night, she typed out her stories. At 4:00 a.m. one morning, word came that her division was moving out. For four years the German army had occupied the capital of France. If all went well, Allied forces would liberate Paris the next day.

Rain fell steadily. At noon the advance halted. As Helen stepped down from her jeep, she slipped and fell. She was certain she had broken her toe. When the advance began again, she gritted her teeth and climbed back into the jeep. She had waited too long for this chance to cover the war in France. A broken toe was not going to stop her from entering Paris with the Allied troops.

That night they camped in a pasture. Helen hopped about on one foot in the mud. In the morning a doctor injected a needle of Novocain into Helen's swollen toe, numbing it. Only then was she able to put on her shoe. [9]

Again the advance began. The rain stopped. The sun came out. It was a good omen.

"I will never forget coming over the hill," said Helen, "and there below was Paris, white and shining in the sun. The American sergeant who was driving was just as excited as we were."

WHAT IS A PRESS CAMP?

A typical press camp during World War II provided living and eating facilities for about fifty war correspondents, both writers and photographers. The facility might be a building, or it might be a tent pitched in a clearing in a field.

The camp was attached to a military unit and moved forward with these combat troops. The camp itself was behind the front lines, though not completely safe from enemy fire. Military officers held "briefings," or updates on military maneuvers, in the press camps. Here, too, correspondents wrote their stories on manual typewriters. When telephone lines were available, correspondents could connect with a bureau office and dictate their handwritten notes. Military censors reviewed all stories and photographs, deleting any references that might prove dangerous to military operations.

HELEN KIRKPATRICK

When Helen was growing up in Rochester, New York, her father took her one day to City Hall. He introduced her to the mayor and explained how city government worked. Often in politics, her father said, there was a "boss." The boss was a person who told others what to do. The boss was not always the one people had elected into office.

Helen's interest in politics and the struggle for power started that day. At Smith College she studied international law. She grad-uated among the highest in her class. In 1931, however, the Great Depression meant jobs were hard to get. In particular, no one in her hometown had a need for a woman who understood international law and could speak French. Helen began writing short newspaper stories, which a former teacher submitted to newspapers. Helen didn't earn any money from those first published pieces. A year after graduation she spoke with Stanley Walker, the managing editor of the *New York Herald Tribune*. He already had one woman on staff, he told her. Her name was Ishbel Ross. Still, he offered Helen a job at fourteen dollars a week. The offer came with a stern warning: "If you have any ideas that you're going to go abroad, forget it. I'd never send a woman abroad."

Helen turned the job down and scraped together enough money to get to Europe. While there, she hunted for jobs as a stringer correspondent, earning enough to pay for her room and meals. She eventually wrote two books on the coming war in Europe. Those books impressed the

Four years earlier refugees had streamed out of the city, fleeing the Nazi troops. They had snarled at traffic, cursed those whose trucks had broken down, slowing their escape. On this day, August 25, 1944, mobs again surged into the streets. They were not fleeing or cursing or begging for help. They were cheering, singing, waving, throwing flowers.

"We were held up, taken out of the jeep, kissed, given wine," Helen said. "It was wild and wonderful."

She made her way to Notre Dame Cathedral, where she managed to climb onto the grill fence, to watch the parade of people cele-brating. She learned that a church service would begin at four o'clock to honor the members of the resistance who had died during the Nazi occupation. Helen eased herself down into the crowd and made her way to one of the cathedral doors.

At 4:15 p.m., General Charles de Gaulle arrived in a jeep. French police had formed a lane, holding back the people, so that the general could enter the church. Suddenly, a revolver shot echoed. Then machine-gun fire peppered the pavement. "The press of the crowd was such that I got shoved into the church," said Helen.

publisher of the *Chicago Daily News*. In 1940, he not only hired Helen to write for him, he sent her to London as a foreign correspondent.

The first story she sent back was an interview with the Duke of Windsor. The duke had refused interviews to reporters from other news publications. Helen had a friend who knew where the duke and duchess were staying in the English countryside. "I went down and saw them," Helen explained later. The duke was gracious but still refused to give Helen the interview. She must have looked terribly disappointed, Helen surmised, because the duke changed his mind. Helen got the interview and sent the story back to Chicago. She had hit the ball out of the park her first time at bat.

During the war Helen first reported on the Nazi Blitz of London. To get close to the action, she often rode in ambulances or on fire trucks during the night bombings. After the D-day invasion of Europe, Helen was never far behind the troops. Helen's war correspondence was so popular back in the States that the *Daily News* called her "Our Helen." When the war ended, Helen received three distinguished awards. The French government awarded her two medals for her writing: the French Legion of Honor and the Médaille de la Reconnaissance. In 1946, the U.S. government awarded her the Medal of Freedom for her war correspondence.

After the war Helen left journalism and accepted a position with the U.S. government. She continued to travel throughout Europe. Eventually, she fell in love and married. She once told an interviewer that she had three careers: "I had journalism. I had government. And I had marriage."

The church interior was dim, lit only by candles. The stained-glass windows shut out the summer sunshine. Helen saw she was only a few feet behind the general. Again machine-gun fire exploded. The man beside Helen fell. Someone pushed Helen forward down the aisle. Now the French police were firing back. A bullet chipped the stone pillar just to her left. Helen was certain she would become one of the victims of a sniper's bullet.

And then it ended. The police apprehended the snipers and marched them away.

The crisis was over. The celebrations continued. Everywhere in Paris, the people partied, crying, *"Vive la France! Vive les Etats-Unis!"*

The next day Helen wrote her story. The *Chicago Daily News* printed it in full with a sensational headline about its star reporter: DAILY NEWS WRITER SEES MAN SLAIN AT HER SIDE IN HAIL OF LEAD. The headline did not refer to Helen Kirkpatrick as a "newshen" or a "paper doll." She was a newswriter, plain and simple. That's just the way she liked it.

Paris was free. Peace seemed so close. Some people predicted the war in Europe would be over by Christmas. They were wrong. And the winter of 1944 would prove to be deadly.

THE LONG WINTER OF 1944

Day after day, rain fell on Paris. The rivers and canals had risen to dangerous levels so that coal barges remained anchored to the banks. Without coal, the French people could not run their factories or heat their homes. Many people wandered aimlessly in the rain. Correspondent Janet Flanner walked among them, watching and listening. Some appeared greatly relieved that liberation had come at last. On the faces of others, Janet saw doubt and disbelief. Had the war really happened? they seemed to be thinking. Were the Nazis really gone?

In her column for *New Yorker* magazine Janet wrote about the rain and the people and a country changed by war. She compared the Nazis to cannibals who fed on the countries they conquered. They ate "the grain, the meat, the oil, the steel, the liberties, the governments and the men" of these countries. The wounds of war required time to heal. Four months after the liberation of Paris, wrote Janet, the wounds were still open and raw.[10]

That winter Europe was cold and hungry. Fresh meat, sausage, and butter were scarce. Availability of gas for cooking, Janet reported, was limited to ninety minutes at noon and one hour between seven and eight o'clock for supper. Most families lived on soup made of carrots and turnips. Even sitting at the table in their homes, they did not remove their damp overcoats. Most families mourned the loss of someone who had died in the war or had been stolen away to work in the labor camps in Germany. Still, despite their sorrow and the cold rain and the watery soup, Janet said, "Paris seems like home for the first time" in many years.[11]

While the rain fell in Paris, snow fell in the Forest of Ardennes. Temperatures dropped below zero. The wind could freeze the flesh on a soldier's unprotected face. Soldiers huddled in frozen foxholes. The cold jammed their weapons and iced the lifesaving containers of blood. Here in the dark forest, the Nazis did not retreat. Hitler mustered his troops and made a powerful show of force that nearly defeated the Allied armies. The fighting lasted for weeks and became known as the Battle of the Bulge. The German army had made a counterattack along the front line. For a time the Allies feared the German troops might break through. The Allied forces held, however, and once again the German army was in retreat.

As the Allies pushed forward through the German countryside, the war correspondents moved with them. Martha Gellhorn was moving with the troops as well. She had crossed from Italy into Germany. She had no military papers or food rations. Often she did not wear her uniform. Still, she took notes and wrote stories. She was on her own. She knew how to link up with other correspondents when she needed to file a story or how to close in behind the troops as they advanced. Because no military officer controlled where she went or what she saw, she saw a part of war that other correspondents did not.

Eventually, the military police caught up with her. They took her to the commanding officer in that area. Martha argued her case. Her job was to write what she saw and heard. But how could she do her job if the military would not let her see anything or talk to anyone? The commanding officer smiled. She'd make an excellent guerrilla soldier, he told her, and he let her go. Once again Martha Gellhorn was on the road and on her own.

In December she interviewed ten American soldiers camped in a gutted farmhouse. "I wouldn't go up that road," a sergeant told her. The Germans were there. "They've got about thirty tanks coming this way."

"What are you going to do?" Martha asked.

"Stay here," one of the soldiers answered.

"We got a gun," said another. [12]

Martha scribbled the conversation into her notebook. She would later weave it into a story she'd write on the Battle of the Bulge.

War was not always about battalions of soldiers invading a country. It was more often about individuals, like this group of ten "unshaven, gaunt-looking" men guarding a lonely road from the enemy. War was not about statistics. It was about people. War was a soldier toasting a cheese sandwich over a small fire in the field. War was a postcard with a baby's picture on it, found near the body of a dead German soldier. War was children sleigh riding on a hill while bombers flew overhead.

Martha had discovered the children on New Year's Day outside the city of Luxembourg. The children were laughing, squealing with delight as their wooden sleds careened downhill through the snow. They did not seem to hear the pounding artillery in the distance. She and the driver she was with stood on the hill and watched. "Children aren't so dumb," the driver said. "What I mean is, children got the right idea. What people ought to do is go coasting." [13]

He and Martha borrowed a sled and went coasting too. That night when he dropped her off at still another military camp, somewhere behind the front lines, he thanked Martha. "I haven't had so much fun since I left home," he told her.

Martha was "heartily sick" of the war, she said. That night she penned a New Year's resolution for the men who ran the world: "Get to know the people who live in it."

INSIDE THE CAMPS

The rain stopped. The snows melted. Paris came back to life in the spring. Men fished again in the Seine River. People gathered at sidewalk cafés and spoke freely without fear of the Gestapo. Fashion models posed for photographers. In the Hotel Scribe, war correspondents typed their stories. The Allied troops had pushed into Holland, Poland, and finally, Germany.

Lee Miller, however, had left Paris and had continued to move forward with the troops. She was confident in her work, and yet she had no way of knowing what her readers at *Vogue* were thinking. In a letter dated December 1944, she wrote to editor Audrey Withers: "I have no way of knowing what you like or what you are using. . . . It could be six weeks before I see what you have published so I barge on, feeling futile, like dropping stones into a well which is so bottomless that there is no returning sound on which to base a calculation." Her editor might have had difficulty getting back to Lee in the field, since the photographer was constantly on the move. If she had succeeded in contacting her, she would have reassured her. *Vogue* was publishing everything—all Lee's words and pictures, even if they were gory or grim. The ladies who read *Vogue* were interested in every detail.

"I want more than anything, to be able to follow the war to the finish over here," Lee wrote to Audrey. Apparently, it was what *Vogue*'s readers wanted as well. [14]

What Lee discovered in Germany angered her. In Nazi-occupied countries the people, including children, truly had been cannibalized, as Janet Flanner had written. The fields had been poisoned by years of war. Bombs had fallen over Germany, too. And yet the German people seemed well nourished. Their cupboards were not bare, she noted. Lee wrote:

> Germany is a beautiful landscape dotted with jewel-like villages. . . . There are blossoms and vistas; every hill is crowned with a castle. The vineyards of the Moselle and the newly ploughed plains are fertile. Immaculate birches and tender willows flank the streams. . . . Little girls in white dresses and garlands promenade after their first communion. The children have stilts and marbles and tops and hoops, and they play with

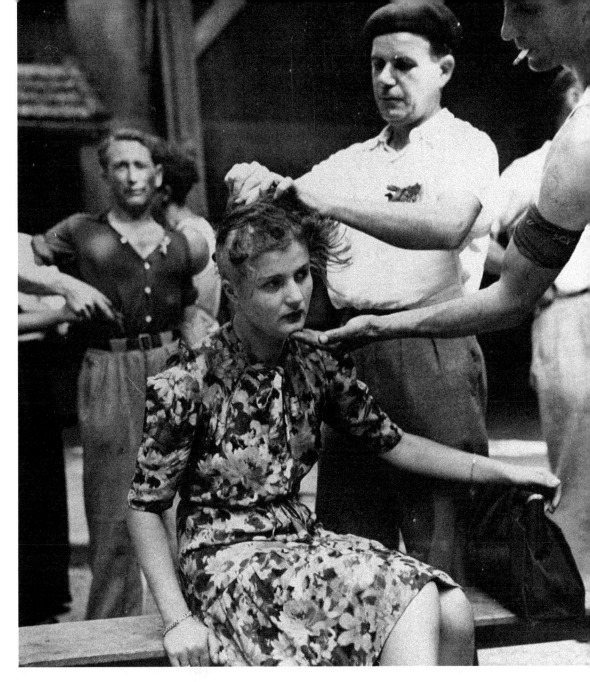

This woman collaborated with the Nazis during the war.
After the war, her fellow citizens publicly humiliated
her for her betrayal by shaving her head.

dolls. Mothers sew and
sweep and bake, and
farmers plough and harrow;
all just like real people.
But they aren't. They are
the enemy. This is Germany
and it is spring. [15]

Surely the war in Europe was nearly over. But the horrors continued. The Allied troops liberated more than cities. They freed prisoners from Gestapo jails. They freed those men and women kidnapped from their homelands and forced to work in slave factories. They freed the inmates of the concentration camps. What they discovered inside these camps was very difficult to believe and impossible to understand.

The stories the correspondents wrote about the camps differed in details. No one could bear writing about *everything* he or she saw. It was too awful. And so they selected details carefully and urged their audiences to believe that what they had written was true.

Radio broadcaster Ed Murrow was among the first inside the camp at Buchenwald. A few days later he began his broadcast with a warning for his listeners: "If you have no appetite to hear what Germans have done, now is a good time to switch off the radio."

Hundreds of thousands had died from starvation, disease, torture, Murrow reported. Those who had survived were too weak to lift their heads from their filthy bunks. Some applauded, Murrow said, as he walked through the barracks. The sound was weak, like baby hands. [16]

General George Patton also struggled with the horror inside Buchenwald. Reportedly, after touring the camp, he got sick to his stomach behind a barracks. Later he ordered the civilians who lived in the nearby town to tour the camp.

Lee Miller photographed the great heap of bodies the Nazis had no time to bury before the Allied troops arrived. She was there when General Patton forced the Germans to view the corpses. Some villagers fainted. Some covered their eyes. The soldiers pulled their hands down and forced them to see what they had allowed to happen.

"We didn't know!" they cried.

"No one in Germany has ever heard of a concentration camp," Lee Miller wrote in her article that accompanied the photographs she sent to *Vogue*. The camp was within walking distance of the town, she argued. How could they not know?

Lee was not alone in stating this. As other war correspondents and photographers pushed forward with the troops, they, too, expressed disbelief. Each asked: How could the German people have allowed this to happen?

The guard tower at the Dachau concentration camp.

DACHAU AND
THE END OF WAR

Marguerite Higgins had spent most of the war as a reporter on the home front. She had always been aggressive in hunting down stories. In the three years she had worked for the *New York Herald Tribune*, she had learned how to ask hard questions. She had begun pressuring her editor to send her to Europe to cover the war. In the spring of 1945, the War Department finally accredited her.

In Paris she teamed up with a reporter for the military newspaper *Stars and Stripes.* Sergeant Peter Furst was a soldier, had a jeep, and could take her where she needed to go to scoop a story on her competitors. She had been inside Buchenwald. Now the Allied forces were moving toward Dachau. She and Peter took another route, hoping that they would be the first reporters there. They drove through country villages where, ten years ago, great flags bearing the swastika hung from storefronts and balconies. Those flags were gone. White banners of surrender hung in their place.

Marguerite and Peter were not only the first reporters at Dachau, they had arrived before the Allied troops. The camp was still under Nazi control. They sat in the jeep and pondered what to do. A guard stood at the gate waving a white banner. But in the watchtowers were soldiers, and they had their guns aimed at the jeep.

Now another man stepped forward. He identified himself as a member of the International Red Cross. Sergeant Furst said American officers were right behind him.

They would arrive at any time. In truth, Marguerite knew it could be hours before the troops arrived. What Marguerite did next surprised even her. She spoke in forceful German to the guards. *"Kommen Sie hier, bitte. Wir sind Amerikaner"*—"Come here, please. We are Americans."

Perhaps they believed Sergeant Furst's bluff. Perhaps they realized the war was lost. Whatever the reason, they gave up their weapons. [17]

Sergeant Furst and Marguerite drove through the gates to where the prisoners were held. Later, in the story she'd write for the *Herald Tribune*, Marguerite described what she had seen. She would win her first journalism award for this story.

The prisoners who rushed toward her at the gates of Dachau that day were "tattered, emaciated . . . weeping and yelling," she wrote. Not all had strength enough to walk, however. Still they made their way toward freedom, crawling. One prisoner, who was a Polish Catholic priest, embraced Marguerite, then pulled back in bewilderment. Why, this "helmeted, uniformed, begoggled individual" was a woman! [18]

Marguerite Higgins was not the only correspondent to walk through the gates of Dachau and witness for herself the crematorium, the torture chambers, the cattle cars, and the ditches that served as mass graves, but she was among the first. Martha Gellhorn arrived a few days later, in early May. Her first sight was of the prisoners, now freed but still too weak to go anywhere. "Behind the barbed wire and the electric fence, the skeletons sat in the sun and searched themselves for lice," she wrote. [19]

Like the other correspondents and military officers and soldiers, Martha walked slowly through the camp. She stopped to interview a Polish doctor caring for the survivors. The doctor told of cruel medical experiments that the Nazi scientists had performed on the inmates. While listening to this new horror, a man entered the infirmary. In a whisper he said the German army had surrendered. The war was over.

Martha should have felt elation, but she did not. The day was sunny, but a darkness had entered her soul, she said. For as long as she would live, Martha Gellhorn would never forget the Nazi concentration camps. [20]

Later she found space on a plane carrying American prisoners of war out of Germany. A soldier thought that perhaps she, too, had been a prisoner. "No," she assured him. "I am only bumming a ride." Then she told him where she had been: Dachau.

"No one will believe us," he said.

Survivors in a crowded Dachau barrack after liberation.

Another soldier spoke. "We've got to talk about it [whether] anyone believes us or not."

Martha coped the only way she knew how—through writing. The final three paragraphs of her article on Dachau were a sort of memorial to the war itself. She had been in Dachau, where the German armies surrendered. She had seen the horrors of concentration camps, which she called "cemetery prisons." How could there be peace in a world where humans committed such cruelty to others? she asked.

She blamed the Allies, in part, for those prisons. The Allied nations had "tolerated" the camps for twelve years. "We were blind and unbelieving and slow, and that we can never be again," she wrote. She ended her article with a warning: "And if ever again we tolerate such cruelty we have no right to peace."[21]

MEET MARGUERITE HIGGINS

Marguerite was born in Hong Kong in September 1920. Her father was an American freight worker. Her mother was French. When she was just six months old, she became seriously ill with malaria, a disease spread by mosquitoes. The doctor recommended that the young parents take their baby to a mountain resort in Dalat, where she might have a better chance of recovery. They did, and soon Marguerite was healthy once again.

Ironically, Dalat was located in Vietnam, a place Marguerite would travel to many times as an older woman and an experienced, award-winning journalist. On her last journey, she would once again become ill from the bite of an insect. This time, however, she would not recover. She died of complications of a rare tropical disease in 1966.

Her life was one of adventure and ambition. Her appearance deceived people. She was beautiful, with large blue eyes the color of sapphires. She was petite and very feminine.

When she applied to graduate school for journalism at Columbia University, the admissions counselor told her the class was filled. Marguerite somehow found a way to be admitted.

When she applied to the *New York Herald Tribune*, the editor at first turned her down. When he finally did hire her, he swore he would not send her overseas. But once again Marguerite got what she wanted. By 1945, she was reporting on the liberation of the concentration camps and won her first journalism award for her story on Dachau. The New York Newspaper Women's Club selected the story as "the best foreign correspondence of 1945."

Her fellow World War II correspondents had strong opinions about her. Janet Flanner, a writer for the *New Yorker*, sailed to Europe on the same ship with Marguerite. Janet thought Marguerite, with her blond hair and sweet smile, looked like Goldilocks of fairy-tale fame. "I wanted to protect her," she said. But Marguerite Higgins was no little girl lost in the woods. As Janet and the rest of the news world would learn later, Marguerite was ambitious and determined to beat the other correspondents—male or female—in getting the story. She also wrote very well.

Marguerite understood that to succeed as a newswriter, she would have to devote herself to her career full-time. That meant no time for a husband or rearing a family. "Of course there were many times when I felt lonely. . . . Aloneness was the price I had to pay in that phase of my life."

In time, however, one phase ended and another began. She met and married her husband, a military officer. She became a mother. Still, she continued to work as a war correspondent. In Korea she learned to carry a carbine. She was a lousy shot, she said. But the enemy didn't know that.

On September 19, 1950, Marguerite Higgins came under enemy fire in Inchon Harbor, on the coast of Korea in the South Pacific. She took shelter in the water beside her assault boat, then "snaked" on her stomach to the rocky seawall. All the while, bullets whizzed over her head and splattered the water around her.

She was not alone. With her were thirty American marines. She was on assignment, covering the U.S. Marines as they attempted to land on "Red Beach." Four waves of troops had already gone ashore. Marguerite was among the fifth wave.

By nightfall the marines had secured the beachhead and Marguerite Higgins was out of the water, safe on the mudflats but not yet dry. She filed her story, describing the landing and experience of being pinned down by enemy fire:

In the sky there was good news. A bright, white star shell from the high ground to our left and an amber cluster told us that the first wave had taken their initial objective, Observatory Hill. But whatever the luck of the first four waves, we were relentlessly pinned down by rifle and automatic weapon fire coming down on us from another rise on the right.

The story ran in the *New York Herald Tribune*, the newspaper that had hired Marguerite Higgins as a "paper doll" during the Second World War. After the war Marguerite had continued to fight for acceptance as a war correspondent. Her story on Inchon Harbor won journalism's highest award, the Pulitzer Prize, in 1951. She was the first woman to win the prize for war correspondence.

In the early 1960s, Marguerite took a position with *Newsday*. Her new assignment was to cover Vietnam, where once again war clouds had darkened the sky. While there, Marguerite contracted a serious illness. Although she returned home to the United States and received care in a military hospital, the disease was too advanced. At the time of Marguerite's death, the petite blonde with cool blue eyes had won more than fifty journalism awards, including the George Polk Memorial Award given by the Overseas Press Club for exceptional courage and enterprise in reporting.

SEPTEMBER 1, 1945

" My fellow Americans, and the Supreme Allied Commander, General MacArthur, in Tokyo Bay: The thoughts and hopes of all America–indeed of all the civilized world–are centered tonight on the battleship *Missouri*. There on that small piece of American soil anchored in Tokyo Harbor the Japanese have just officially laid down their arms. They have signed terms of unconditional surrender... "

*PRESIDENT HARRY S. TRUMAN, BROADCAST FROM THE WHITE HOUSE AT 10 P.M.

Chapter Seven

VICTORY
IN THE
SOUTH PACIFIC

When did Adolf Hitler realize he had lost the war? Not during the D-day invasion. He had always expected the Allies to invade France one day. Not during the Battle of the Bulge. His panzers had nearly defeated the Allies in the Ardennes Forest. Even when more than one hundred thousand German men had been killed, wounded, or were missing during that bitter winter of 1944, Hitler still believed he would be the victor.

Early in 1945, he told a trusted officer that if Germany should lose the war, he would die with his troops. And yet even then, he spoke of a secret weapon his scientists were building. This atomic bomb, he said, would pulverize England's cliffs of Dover, sending them to the bottom of the sea.

In mid-April, Allied troops surrounded Berlin. Behind them came an army of war correspondents, both male and female. Among them were Lee Miller, Marguerite Higgins, and Helen Kirkpatrick.

Hitler learned that his officers were no longer following his orders. Perhaps then he understood that all was lost. In those final days, however, Hitler never admitted he had failed. The country, he said, was weak. "[Germany] was not quite ready or quite strong enough for the mission I set for the nation," he said. [1]

On May 1, 1945, German radio announced, "Our Führer . . . has died a hero's death." He did not die in battle as the radio propaganda suggested. Alone, in his room, Adolf Hitler ended his own life.

LEE MILLER AND HITLER'S BATHTUB

On the day Adolf Hitler died, Lee Miller took a leisurely bath in the dictator's tub in Munich, Germany. She had been traveling with fellow photographer David E. Scherman. They had arrived in Munich with the Allied troops. Lee and David, as well as some officers, had moved into the führer's private house for a few days.

The memory of the living skeletons in the concentration camp was fresh in Lee's mind, and in David's, too. They were tired and they were depressed. The news that the man who had caused such misery was dead might have been reason for celebration. They decided instead to stage a photograph in the führer's green-tiled bathroom.

Lee drew the bathwater. She and David arranged objects in the room. They set a photograph of Hitler on the lip of the tub. They placed Lee's muddy combat boots on a dirty bath mat near the tub. In the final photograph only Lee's head and bare shoulders can be seen as she sits in the bath. She holds a washcloth to her neck. She is not smiling. Rather, she is looking over her shoulder with grim determination. While she posed, David shot the photograph. Outside the locked bathroom door, an officer demanded they hurry up. He wanted a shower.

What does the photograph mean? Why would Lee and David make such an image? Years later her son, Antony, proposed an answer. The photograph was, he believes, one of Lee's favorites because "it gave her a sense of victory over an evil man," he said.

Born in 1907 in Poughkeepsie, New York, Lee

Just two weeks earlier in Warm Springs, Georgia, Franklin Delano Roosevelt had complained of a terrible headache. Minutes later he collapsed. Doctors were not able to revive him. The president had died of a stroke.

Roosevelt's health had been deteriorating, but his death shocked the world. "But the war is almost over!" cried a soldier aboard a troopship. Winston Churchill, the prime minister of England, broke down in tears when announcing the president's death at the House of Commons.

These two men, so different and so powerful, had come into office in the same year. Now they had died within days of each other. The free world joined America in grieving the death of FDR. Few grieved for Adolf Hitler.

When Germany surrendered, the war in Europe ended. But fighting still continued in the South Pacific.

Miller learned early the power of photographs. She began her work in photography in front of the camera as a model. She posed for magazine advertisements. As a young woman of twenty-two, she traveled to Paris and became the model for artist Man Ray. She also became his pupil. He taught her not only how to use camera equipment but also composition—that is, how to arrange the elements within the camera's frame. She learned quickly and well and eventually established her own photographic studio.

When the Second World War began, she was living in England. She was a photographer for *Vogue* magazine. She received her accreditation in 1944. She photographed the field hospitals and later followed the troops as they pushed forward through France and Germany. Lee Miller never suffered any serious wounds aside from some bruises and scrapes.

After the war, however, she suffered emotionally from what she had seen. A few years later she put away her cameras and devoted herself to her new husband and her son. She developed a passion for gardening. She never spoke of the war again. She was often depressed, however. Today, medical experts might have diagnosed her with a condition called "post-traumatic stress disorder." A person who suffers from this disorder often relives painful experiences through nightmares. They may have difficulty sleeping or abuse alcohol. In the 1950s and 1960s, doctors did not know about this illness.

Despite the emotional scars of witnessing war, Lee Miller believed her photographs were important historical documents. Her son believes she would be proud to know that historians, art students, and photojournalists still study her images. She died in 1977.

THE WHITE ANGEL

Dickey Chapelle was not as experienced a photographer as Margaret Bourke-White or Lee Miller. She was young, and her work had appeared in just a few magazines. Still, she had managed to convince Fawcett Publications to hire her to report on the war. They published a number of magazines, including *Mechanix Illustrated* and *Family Circle*. When Dickey's accreditation came through, her editor sent her to the South Pacific with this order: "Be sure you're the first someplace."

Dickey flew first to Honolulu, on the Hawaiian island of Oahu. This island was where the war had begun three years ago when the Japanese attacked Pearl Harbor. The harbor was once again an active military port. Many correspondents were stationed here

Dickey Chapelle always wore pearl earrings, even when on the most dangerous war assignments.

Iwo Jima—that's where she wanted to go. The military officer in charge approved orders for Dickey to travel on the USS *Samaritan*. The hospital ship was departing at five in the morning on a mission to transport the wounded of Iwo Jima back to Guam. Dickey's assignment while aboard was to document the use of whole blood in saving lives. Dickey would not only be the first someone someplace, but she'd also be the only photographer aboard.

The *Samaritan* was as large as a city block, Dickey said. Red crosses painted on her deck clearly indicated she was a hospital ship and carried no weaponry, even for her own defense. Smaller, armed ships escorted her. Two days out, the ship came under enemy fire. In her autobiography, which she wrote many years later, Dickey described her fear the moment the ship's Klaxon alarm sounded. She hurried on deck with her camera. She saw the enemy plane, and then what seemed to be nothing but "a dark speck" falling from the plane. It was a bomb. The pilot had released it too soon, however. It didn't strike the *Samaritan*. Now Dickey threw herself flat on the deck, her camera in position, ready for the pilot to make a second run and a second attempt to strike. She focused her lens. In her viewfinder the plane grew larger as it approached. Her hands began to tremble. This was it. This was war.

along with troops. Dickey got military permission to go forward, to the island of Guam. "This marked the first break-through of American women in the armed forces to a post of duty forward of Honolulu," she said. But Dickey wasn't content. The real story was the fierce fighting on the island of Iwo Jima. For days American marines had been fighting a desperate battle against the Japanese entrenched on the island. The number of wounded and dead was staggering.

Dickey Chapelle, on assignment with the marines in South Vietnam in the 1960s, wades through a swamp.

Suddenly a navy destroyer escorting the *Samaritan* fired on the enemy plane. Dickey watched as the pilot "turned tail and fled."

She *watched*. She did not photograph.

Shaken, she heard again the words her husband had told her when teaching her photography: "The picture is your reason for being. It doesn't matter what you've seen with your eyes. If you can't prove it happened with a picture, it didn't happen."[2]

Dickey felt miserable. She had failed on her first time out.

The marines made up grisly names for the battles they fought. "Death Valley" and "Meat Grinder" suggested the terrible loss of life in combat on islands in the South Pacific. Once the *Samaritan* anchored in the waters off Iwo Jima, Dickey came up with a name of her own. A Samaritan is a person who eases the suffering of others. Every person aboard the hospital ship was a Samaritan. So

Dickey Chapelle photographed this wounded soldier aboard the USS *Samaritan*. Although seriously wounded, he would survive.

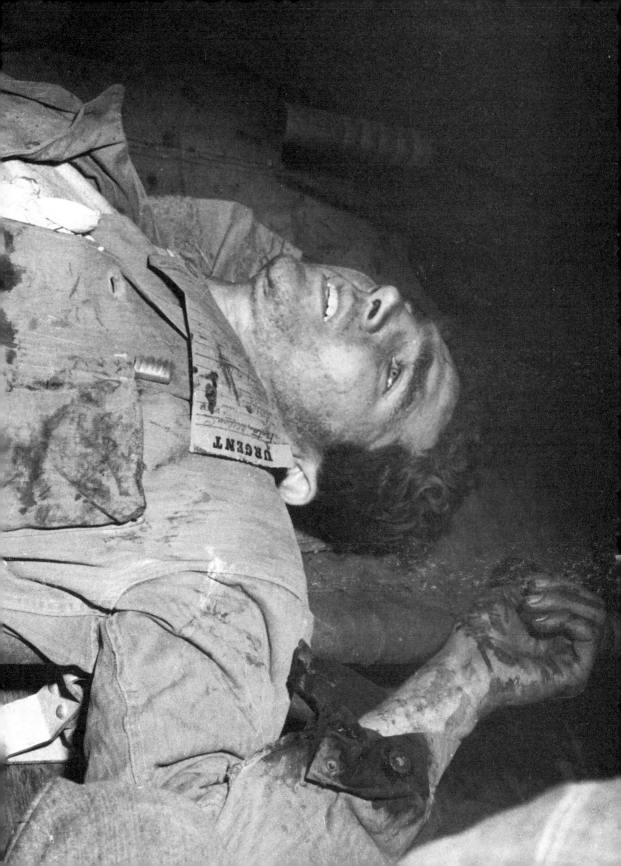

Dickey started referring to the ship itself as the "White Angel."

Within hours, wounded lay side by side on the ship's well deck. Dickey tried to keep out of the way of the nurses and orderlies on deck. She tried also not to slip and fall in the blood. Nothing she had ever seen or done in her life before had prepared her for this day. The camera was like a wall, separating her from the wounded. Dickey worked quickly. She framed each subject in her viewfinder, then adjusted the lens and snapped the photograph. Quickly, she recorded each soldier's identification number—engraved on his "dog tag"—in her notebook. Then she moved on to the next casualty.

When her camera ran out of film, Dickey squatted on the deck to reload. As her fingers worked, she glanced at a bloody bundle lying on a stretcher beside her. The soldier wore a tag that read URGENT. Painted on his forehead was a large *M*. The *M* stood for "morphine." A medic on the beach had injected the powerful drug into the soldier in order to dull the wounded man's pain. In the last few hours Dickey had seen many wounded labeled in this same way. As long as she refused to think of the bloody bundles as real people, she could continue photographing. But something happened in those few moments while she changed film.

"I hadn't looked at the faces of any hurting man except through the viewfinder of the camera," she said. "Now, shyly, without the square of glass between us, I looked at him."

He was smiling at her. Dickey lowered her camera. She could not look away. He wasn't a shapeless, dirty green bundle at all. He was a young man. Her understanding of war changed in that moment. The war was not about numbers or the names of beaches and battles. The bloody bundles were real people who had risked their lives so that others might live.

"What's your name?" she asked. "Where are you from?"

"Scranton," he told her, a small coal-mining town in northeastern Pennsylvania.

For a few minutes more Dickey stayed with him. Martin was the first soldier with whom Dickey connected personally. In lowering her camera and seeing him, really looking at him, she had stepped out of the safe territory of regarding the wounded as "bloody green bundles" and into the dangerous realm of understanding that they were men.

"After that," she said, "I looked squarely at each marine as I photographed him."[3]

That day Dickey understood her purpose for being aboard the "White Angel." She was the only one there to tell Martin's story, to tell the stories of all the marines who were sacrificing their lives. Now as she moved from one stretcher to another, she spoke with the marines. They told her little bits about themselves. Many felt lucky. Some were angry and cursed the war. Many more worried about their buddies, still on the beach or fighting in the jungles. Dickey began to understand why these marines were fighting. It was not, as she had imagined, for the people back home. It was for one another, their buddies.

In a quiet moment late that night, Dickey wrote a letter to her husband. She feared she was not strong enough to be a war correspondent. Alone on her cot, she could still smell the dust from the hundreds of plastic casts made that day. She could still hear the anxious shouts and grunts of the corpsmen lifting the wounded from the water ambulances to the deck. She could still hear the cries of those so terribly wounded.

"I am not able to do it, Tony," she wrote. [4]

Dickey overcame her self-doubt. She did not curl into a ball on her cot, as perhaps she had wanted to. Early the next morning she loaded her camera and continued her work. Afraid she might faint while photographing operations, she tied herself with ropes to the pipes. Later she searched the bunks for the men she had photographed the day before. Some had not made it. Many more did. She ran her finger over the dog tag numbers until she came to Martin's. When she tracked him down, she smiled. He had survived.

With more than seven hundred wounded aboard, the USS *Samaritan* steamed away from the terrible fighting on Iwo Jima and headed for Guam. Those days aboard the ship were Dickey's first close-up encounter with war. Many years later she would write in her autobiography what she had learned about those who fight wars:

> I believe a man goes into combat for the defense of the folks back home. But no country, no slogan, no edict, no law, no global pronouncement, no parliamentary decision is ever what he dies for. He dies for the man on his right or his left. He dies exposing himself so that they or all of them may live, often in that order. Greater love hath no man. And there isn't any other word. [5]

DICKEY CHAPELLE

Georgette Louise Meyer was born in Shorewood, Wisconsin, in 1919. When she was a little girl, her father took her to air shows where stunt pilots buzzed the bleachers and made death-defying dives. "Georgie Lou," as her friends called her, had a dream. One day she would learn to fly. Her mother, however, was terrified of airplanes. She made her young daughter promise she would never step into an airplane. Georgie Lou never gave up her fascination with flying. One of her best-loved Christmas presents was a book her father gave her when she was sixteen called *Simple Aerodynamics.*

In time one dream replaced another. By the time she had graduated with honors from high school, Georgie Lou had decided that she'd become an aeronautical engineer. She would design her own airplanes. She won a scholarship to one of the best schools for science and engineering in the country, the Massachusetts Institute of Technology (MIT).

Her childhood hero had been Admiral Richard E. Byrd, who in 1929 became the first American to reach the South Pole. Calling herself "Dickey" after her hero, she left home for MIT in 1935 fully intending to do as the admiral had done: to set a nearly impossible goal and do everything in her power to achieve it. Her admittance to MIT was itself an achievement—she was one of only seven women admitted to the college that year.

Dickey was intelligent. She had graduated from high school a year earlier than her classmates. At MIT, however, her grades were poor. She cut classes in order to spend time at the nearby coast guard base or the navy yard in Boston to watch the airplanes. She hung around the mechanics and learned how to use special tools built for airplane engines. She broke the promise she had made to her mother years ago and took her first flight aboard an airplane. The classroom was boring in comparison to the activity at the air bases. During her sophomore year at MIT, Dickey's grades slipped even more. One day the dean called her into his office. The school was taking away her scholarship, he told her. Dickey had flunked out of college.

While at MIT, she had earned money by writing articles on airplanes and flying for local magazines. Although Dickey returned home to Wisconsin for a short time, she eventually decided to move to New York City, where she might find work as a writer. In New York she enrolled in a photography course. Her teacher was Tony Chapelle. He had been a photographer during World War I. Tony thought Dickey was one of his best students. He encouraged her to pursue photography rather than writing. Although Tony was older and had been married once before, he and Dickey fell in love and married.

On Sunday afternoon, December 7, 1941, the newlyweds were driving along the Hudson River in New York when the radio announcer interrupted the program with a news flash. Japan had bombed

American military ships and planes at Pearl Harbor. Tony pulled the car to the side of the road. Together, he and Dickey listened to the incredible news that America was now at war. As an experienced combat photographer, Tony could easily get military accreditation as a photojournalist. Dickey had begun selling photographs to magazines, but she was young and inexperienced. She still had much to learn. Even so, Dickey was determined that she, too, would become a war correspondent.

The war separated the Chapelles, as it separated many young couples. Tony worked for the Office of War Information in New York. Dickey's military accreditation, however, took her halfway around the world to the South Pacific. During the war Dickey showed grit in getting her story no matter the risks. She broke military restrictions and nearly lost her credentials by hitching a ride "to the front" on the island of Okinawa. Dickey recalled hearing the buzz of bullets over her head as she snapped photographs. A furious general finally located her in the jungle among the troops and ordered her back to her ship.

After the war Dickey continued her career as a photographer. She often felt her work wasn't as good as that of the more famous photojournalist Margaret Bourke-White. Because of this, Dickey pushed herself hard. An editor at *National Geographic* once said of Dickey's work, "She would stick with a story two or three months while another reporter would stay two days. And she would bring back the facts, no matter how long it would take."

Her dedication to her career might have been one reason why her marriage to Tony ended in divorce.

In the early 1960s, when she was forty years old, Dickey Chapelle learned how to parachute from an airplane. American forces were once again fighting a war, this time in a small Asian country called Vietnam. There was no front line in this war. Instead, the method of fighting was called "guerrilla warfare." Small combat groups roamed through the thick jungles. An ambush or a firefight could erupt at any time. The enemy often hid in a network of tunnels dug throughout the mountains. Dickey decided the best way to get her story was to parachute into the jungle where the American marines were fighting. Dickey became the first female photographer the War Department (now known as the Pentagon) approved to jump with the troops.

As a child, Dickey had dreamed of doing something as heroic and meaningful as her hero, Admiral Byrd. She did not plant the American flag on the South Pole as he had, but she earned a place for herself in journalism and women's history through her combat experiences. In 1965, while on patrol with marines in Vietnam, a land mine exploded. Bits of metal cut into Dickey's neck. The marines evacuated her by helicopter to a field hospital. She died before the helicopter touched down.

Dickey Chapelle was not the first journalist to die in war. She was, however, the first woman journalist who had given her life while covering her country's troops in battle.

SHELLEY'S RETURN
TO THE SOUTH PACIFIC

Throughout the spring and summer of 1945, American forces recaptured one island after another in the South Pacific. Shelley and Carl Mydans returned to that area, but they were no longer a roving husband-and-wife team. *Life* **assigned Carl to General MacArthur as the troops advanced across the South Pacific. Shelley followed behind, reporting on the surrender of the Japanese on the islands.**

On Guam she reported on thirty-three ragged soldiers who had come down from the mountains into a clearing to give themselves up. The U.S. Marines had taken Guam many months earlier, but these Japanese soldiers had hidden in the jungle. As Shelley reported, Colonel Howard Stent told the Japanese, "You are now prisoners of war. This is no disgrace." The Japanese men, wrote Shelley, turned east toward the direction of Japan and their emperor. "They bowed, eyes closed," she wrote. "Then they went off to the prisoners' stockade."

She herself had been a POW for twenty-one months, but Shelley did not write what she felt at that moment. As a correspondent, her personal feelings had no place in a news article.

And yet Shelley was the subject of another article. The correspondent's name was not given, but he was a male, as most war correspondents were. He wrote with admiration about Shelley. He called her "the Pacific's first gorgeous war correspondent." But, he added, a single sentence could never describe Shelley. She was an "able newspaperwoman," he wrote, who knew more about their Japanese enemies than most military commanders knew. In the often horrific world of war, Shelley Mydans never panicked. He admired that quality about her. [6]

> **A dense column of smoke rises more than 60,000 feet above the port of Nagasaki, Japan, as the result of an atomic explosion. Three days earlier, the United States had dropped an atomic bomb on the Japanese city of Hiroshima.**

"RAIN OF RUIN"

Just as Hitler had not accepted defeat and fought to the very last, so too were the Japanese determined not to surrender. The secret weapon—the atom bomb—Adolf Hitler had spoken about to his trusted officer was a weapon the United States had also been developing. The new president of the United States was Harry S. Truman. He struggled with a terrible decision—whether to invade Japan and risk the loss of thousands of American lives or to drop the atomic bomb and in doing so, kill innocent Japanese civilians. In a letter to his wife, Bess, dated for July 20, 1945, the new president wrote: ". . . I want peace—world peace and will do what can be done by us to get it."

The first-ever use of an atomic weapon would surely bring the Japanese enemy to its knees and end the war. Still, President Truman struggled with what he called the hardest decision of life. Five days later in his diary he wrote about the atomic bomb. "It seems to be the most terrible thing ever discovered, but it can be made the most useful."[7] Perhaps what the president meant was that despite the bomb's fearsome power to obliterate a city and its people, the display of such force might truly put an end not just to the Second World War, but all war.

In August 1945, he authorized the use of this most powerful, most destructive bomb on the city of Hiroshima, Japan. No war correspondents, male or female, were aboard the bomber that flew the mission over Hiroshima. Nor were any on the ground to witness the blinding flash, the violent wind that roared across the city, or the huge mushroom cloud that rose into the sky above the city. The explosion reduced hundreds of buildings to ash. Thousands of people died or were terribly burned.

President Truman presented the leaders of Japan with an ultimatum. "If they do not now accept our terms they may expect a rain of ruin from the air, the like of which has never been seen on this earth."[8]

Japan remained silent.

Days later the Americans dropped a second atomic bomb on Nagasaki.

The president had not exaggerated. In an instant this second blast, like the first, leveled city blocks. For days afterward, a poisonous rain fell on Japan. "The force from which the sun draws its power has been loosed against those who brought war to the Far East," the president said in a statement to the American people.[9]

The two atomic bombs brought Japan to its knees. The leaders agreed to the surrender terms. The Second World War had ended, but the world itself would never be the same again.

The atomic explosion leveled most of the city of Hiroshima. One month after the explosion, the land remains barren and bleak.

"THE STORY IS OVER"

Throughout the four long years of war, Eleanor Roosevelt had continued her Monday-morning press conferences for the ladies of the press. Some of those ladies, like Ruth Cowan and Mary Craig, had secured accreditation and gone overseas to cover the war. Many more remained at home, writing about the war effort on the home front. After the death of the president, however, Mrs. Roosevelt was no longer the nation's First Lady. President Harry Truman had taken the oath of office, and he and his wife, Bess, were moving into the White House.

The former First Lady had packed the president's and her own belongings into hundreds of crates. On Friday she would leave the White House for good. Today, however, she was hosting a farewell tea in the State Dining Room of the White House for her "press girls." Fifty-seven newspaperwomen attended. As she had always done, Mrs. R. shook each woman's hand as they entered the room, but she was not her smiling, exuberant self. She introduced Mrs. Bess Truman to her girls. But it was unlikely that the new First Lady would follow in Mrs. R's footsteps. Bess Truman was not just shy. She believed a woman's first obligation was to her husband and her family.

As the nation's First Lady, her beliefs did not change. She had no desire to meet with the press and be the subject of their news stories.

So, after twelve years, there would be no more Monday-morning press conferences upstairs at the White House. The door that Eleanor Roosevelt had opened for women journalists had closed.

"What will you do now?" one of the women reporters asked Mrs. Roosevelt.

She told them she was moving into an apartment in New York City, where she hoped to live a more quiet life. One of the women reporters noted that Mrs. R's hands were shaking. "This is a social thing," Eleanor said. "Not a press conference. If you want to say 'Mrs. Roosevelt said this or that in conversation,' that is your privilege, but I do not want to be quoted directly."

In a drizzling rain the next day, Mrs. Roosevelt left the White House. A black limousine drove her to Union Station. By evening the former First Lady had arrived at her home in New York City. Reporters were waiting in the street. Ordinarily, she would have stopped and chatted. She had never turned away from the press. This day, however, she said simply, "The story is over."[10]

But the story wasn't over, not yet.

"MY DAY" BY ELEANOR ROOSEVELT

Throughout the twelve years that Eleanor Roosevelt had been First Lady of the United States, she had continued to write her newspaper column "My Day." She began writing the column in 1935 as a way to share some of her ideas and experiences with the American people, particularly with women readers. Like her Monday-morning press conferences, the column was intended as a way to express her ideas about social rather than political matters. The column appeared six days a week, which meant that in addition to her duties as First Lady, Eleanor Roosevelt also had a daily deadline to meet.

A review of her column during the war years provides an interesting window to the social issues that most concerned the First Lady. Civil rights, working women, the persecution of Jewish people in Europe—all were topics on which she wrote. Through her words, too, her readers saw a side of her that ordinarily might have been hidden. They knew, for example, the First Lady often stood at her bedroom window to gaze at the Washington Monument before going to sleep. "The little red light at the top of it has twinkled at me in friendly fashion," she once wrote in a column. They learned, too, that if she were younger she might have volunteered to serve as a nurse during the war with the army or navy, but that she cherished being a housewife above all else.

On April 21, 1945, she wrote about her last day in the White House. She had breakfasted on the sun porch. At four o'clock she met for the last time with her Monday-morning press girls. She escorted the new First Lady, Bess Truman, on a tour of the White House.

Although no longer America's First Lady, Eleanor Roosevelt remained active in political and social welfare activities. She served as the United States representative to the United Nations. President John Kennedy appointed her in the early 1960s to serve on a committee investigating the status of women. "My Day" might have ended with Eleanor's departure from the White House and the nation's capital. But the former First Lady had earned so much respect and admiration among her readers that newspapers continued to publish her column until her death in 1962. When she died, flags across country flew at half-mast to honor her.

Martha Gellhorn first met Eleanor Roosevelt when she was young woman. The First Lady was fifty. The two women, despite the differences in their ages, remained friends for all of their lives. "She gave off light," Martha Gellhorn once wrote about her. "No one seeing her could fail to be moved."

> **In all my reporting life I have thrown small pebbles into a very large pond, and I have no way of knowing whether any pebble caused the slightest ripple. I don't need to worry about that. . . . My responsibility was the effort.**

★MARTHA GELLHORN

Chapter Eight

RETURN
TO NORMALCY?

. . . in all my reporting life I have thrown small pebbles into a very large pond, and I have no way of knowing whether any pebble caused the slightest ripple. I don't need to worry about that. . . . My responsibility was the effort. I belong to a global fellowship, of men and women, who are concerned with the welfare of the planet, and its least protected inhabitants. —Martha Gellhorn

Without a war, there is no need for war correspondents. When the Second World War ended, Toni Frissell returned to America and once again began to photograph celebrities and fashion models for glossy magazines. Lee Miller, too, gave up her military credentials. At home in England, she packed her war gear in a trunk and stored it in the attic. She never spoke of the war again. She married and had a son, Antony. Antony did not know his mother had been a war correspondent until the day he found her trunk in the attic. Inside were her photographs, loose sheets of typed manuscripts, and maps of France still caked with mud. Martha Gellhorn once compared war to disease that causes pain "beyond telling or imagining." Perhaps that is why Lee Miller locked away her memories of war.

Anne O'Hare McCormick had spent a good deal of the Second World War in America. Now she returned to Europe to report on the efforts to rebuild lives as well as cities. In a town in Germany, she watched a woman sweeping the street with a broom. It seemed "futile," Anne wrote. Sweeping away chunks of wood and concrete and rivers of brick dust was not easy. Bulldozers, not brooms, were needed to clear away "the mess men had made." But the woman swept with determination nonetheless. [1]

In Holland and France and Belgium, she saw other women with brooms, each working hard to make their destroyed homes and cities clean again. Some tied the long-legged chrysanthemums outside their homes to stakes. Although the cities were in ruins, the flowers had survived and were once again in bloom. So many husbands and fathers and brothers had died on the battlefields and in concentration camps during the war. But their widows and daughters and sisters were not defeated. They were starting anew, just like the chrysanthemums. The women with brooms gave Anne O'Hare McCormick hope for the world's future.

DEAR SHELLEY ...

On the night before Gene Smith was to go on a combat photography mission for *Life* magazine, he wrote a letter to his fellow war correspondent, Shelley Mydans. He had volunteered for an assignment on the island of Okinawa. He asked Shelley for a special favor. He was frightened, he said. But then, most soliders and war correspondents are when facing the enemy. The favor he asked was a simple one, really. If he lived and the film arrived safely, would Shelley contact his family to tell them that he was okay? [2]

During the night attack, Gene was wounded—but not critically. Likely, Shelley fulfilled Gene's request to let his family know he had survived. To Gene Smith, Shelley Mydans was not a "newshen." She was a colleague who had taken many of the same risks he had in covering the war. The world still typically thought of war correspondents as male, and so they were. But during the Second World War, women correspondents like Shelley Mydans had planted seeds of change. It would take many years more for those seeds to root and grow, but grow they would.

BACK TO THE SOCIETY PAGE

During the Great Depression, the United Press news service hired its first woman correspondent, Ruby Black, to cover Mrs. Roosevelt's Monday-morning press conferences. During the Second World War, the UP hired many more women to fill the jobs of men who had gone to war. Marjorie Bowers Paxson was one of those news reporters. At the time, she signed an agreement that said she would give up her job when the man she was replacing returned.

Thousands of newswomen across the country had signed similar agreements. You had to understand the mood of the country during wartime, said Marjorie. Signing that paper was the patriotic thing to do. Giving up your job once the war ended was also patriotic, or so the newspaper stories and radio broadcasts suggested. The government was urging the country to "return to normalcy."

But what was "normalcy"? Was it the way of life in the 1930s during the Great Depression? Surely no one wanted to go back to the days of breadlines. Was it the way of life in the 1920s before Black Tuesday and the stock market crash? No one wanted to make those mistakes again. Normalcy was different things to different people.

During the war butter fat was needed to make weapons. Normalcy was pats of butter served once again in restaurants.

During the war gasoline and rubber for car tires had been scarce. Normalcy was traffic on city streets and country roads.

During the war factories had produced Liberty ships, fighter planes, and munitions. Normalcy was a return to manufacturing automobiles and other goods for Americans to purchase. Normalcy was employing men, not women, to make those products. Most women untied their bandannas and stepped out of their factory overalls. They went home to cook supper. So did the women who had run the trolleys and the trains.

Likewise, paper dolls across the country gave up their typewriters as they had agreed to do. Normalcy in the newsroom was a return to the days of labeling women as "newshens." Some women kept their jobs, but their assignments shifted from front-page news back to the women's pages again.

The *Chicago Sun* did not require its paper dolls to sign an agreement to give up their jobs once the war ended. That is what happened nevertheless. Isabelle Shelton was one of the *Sun's* paper dolls. In the last months of the war nine women reporters worked for the newspaper. Once the war ended, only

Martha Gellhorn began her career as a war correspondent in Spain in 1937. She would continue to report on wars through the 1980s.

two remained. Isabelle was one of the two. She didn't think she was a better journalist than the other girls. She was just lucky, she said.

Isabelle got even luckier. She fell in love. Because her husband worked in Washington, DC, Isabelle had to give up her job anyway. She moved to the nation's capital to be with him. Almost twenty years earlier, Frances Lide had arrived in Washington confident that she could land a job on Newspaper Row. Isabelle, too, was sure she'd find a job. Day after day, she applied for work with news organizations. Always the answer was the same: We've hired the men who have returned from the war.

Finally, she landed a job in the Washington office of the *Cincinnati Enquirer*. She got it by agreeing to work part of the time as a secretary to one of the feature editors. Her boss paid little attention to her newswriting experience. Instead, he expected his secretary to pour his morning and afternoon coffee and to file his papers. Part of the time Isabelle could still write news, but not just any news. The paper had assigned her to a weekly column called "Society Notes of Washington."

"I was appalled," Isabelle said. "It was nowhere in my area of interest."

In Chicago during the war Isabelle had written about local and state government. She hung out in city hall to scoop stories. She traveled with state senators on their reelection campaigns. She attended school board meetings. In Washington, however, her beat was ladies' tea parties and charity balls.

Still, Isabelle needed a job, and this was the best she could get. She was certain she'd be bored to pieces. Then a fellow "newshen" gave her an idea. The editors didn't know what interested a woman, her friend said. That was up to Isabelle to decide. "You can make almost anything out of this job," her friend said.

Washington is the heart of American politics. Isabelle figured out a way to cover political and social issues while at the same time writing about women. It was just a matter of *which* women to write about! "I interviewed all the women elected to Congress. There weren't that many, but I did stories on all of them," she said. Next, she hunted down the wives of senators and representatives and interviewed them. She went to foreign embassies and spoke with women from different countries who had traveled to America with their husbands. Any woman who was doing something different or interesting became a possible news feature for her "Society Notes."

If Isabelle could not change the newspaper's policy that women worked on women's pages, then she'd just have to change the women's page itself.

THE FLIGHT FROM FLUFF

In the years following the Second World War, Denise McCluggage was one of the lucky college graduates who got a job on a local newspaper. After a few years, however, she left the newspaper in San Francisco and traveled to New York City. She had greater ambitions. In particular, she had set her sights on the *New York Herald Tribune* because Marguerite Higgins worked for that newspaper. In fact, over the years, the *Tribune* had hired quite a few women reporters, among them Emma Bugbee and Ishbel Ross. Now they took a chance on Denise as well.

Like Isabelle Shelton and hundreds of other women newswriters in this period after the war, Denise made the best of the women's page assignments she got. One of her feature stories was on skiing, a sport favored by many well-to-do women. The sports editor at the *Tribune* liked it so much, he convinced the editors to move Denise to his department, and the young reporter could not have been happier. Denise became one of the few women sportswriters in the country at that time. But that wasn't why she was thrilled with her new assignment. She simply loved sports. As a girl, she had sprained her ankles and fingers while playing football and baseball with the boys. As an adult, she especially loved car racing. She had no hesitation in slipping behind the wheel of a race car in order to add excitement to her story for her readers. She soon got a reputation as "the tomboy behind the typewriter."

During the war women correspondents had faced roadblocks but had found ways around them. After the war the roadblocks were still there. Sporting officials "skirted" Denise from the all-male press boxes. Race officials at the Indianapolis 500 car race in 1956 barred her from the pit and garage areas, where the drivers were and where the reporters got their interviews.

"It was silly," she said. "No matter that I was reporting for the *Tribune*. To them, I was a woman, not a reporter. So I just did what I could do, reported from wherever I could." She got her Indianapolis 500 story by interviewing the drivers through a hole in the fence!

The same thing happened during the World Series in New York City. When Denise couldn't get into the press box, she wandered the grandstands. The stuff of her feature story was the conversations of the fans that she had overheard. This determination to succeed despite the roadblocks and the prejudices was something women correspondents had learned to do during the Second World War, during the Great Depression and the years before that.

Something *was* different, however. The seeds of change women writers had planted in these earlier years had taken root and had begun to grow. In other newspapers in other cities, women writers were tackling topics that were untraditional for the women's and society pages. When the *Chicago Daily News* hired Georgie Anne

Marguerite Higgins meets with General Douglas McArthur in Korea in the 1950s. Soon after, she was readmitted to the war zone to report the news.

MARTHA GELLHORN

When the Second World War ended, Martha Gellhorn did not return to the island of Cuba, where she had once lived with her husband, Ernest Hemingway. Their marriage had not been completely happy before the war. The war separated them. Hemingway had also gone to Europe to write about the war, but he and Martha were never together. She went off on her own, reporting from as close to the front lines as she could get. When the war ended, so did their marriage.

Martha returned to England. She said the war had filled her heart with a terrible sorrow. Especially horrifying to her were the concentration camps. She knew she could not stay for long in London unless she found work. Somehow she had to pull herself out of her sorrow. She needed a new assignment, a new challenge. And so she sat down and made a list for herself of things to do and things not to do. On the "not to do" list she wrote: "Ignore for now job problem, money problem, and personal future." On the "to do" list she wrote: "Think of myself as someone new."[3]

Martha had always been self-disciplined. She did not wait for a magazine or a book publisher to come to her. She thought up her own story ideas, then went to them. She did not wait for an editor to pay her way to another country where an important story might be unfolding. The first war she had covered was in Spain, and she had traveled to that country alone with a knapsack, a duffel bag filled with tin cans of food, and her last fifty dollars. Once more Martha disciplined herself to write.

Three months later the "new" Martha Gellhorn had outlined a novel based on her war experiences and had written some short stories. She convinced an American publication, the *New Republic*, to pay her to write travel articles. After months of solitude and sadness Martha was writing and earning money again. She rewarded herself with a return trip to America and a long vacation with her mother.

Martha's self-discipline and fierce independence came from both her mother and her father. She was born in St. Louis, Missouri, in 1909. Her father was a doctor. Her mother had fought for women's rights, including the right to vote. By the time she was eight, Martha heard other children talking about her mother. Many people in 1916 thought suffragists were rebels, and Martha's mother was certainly a suffragist. As a young woman, Martha went to the same college from which her mother had graduated, Bryn Mawr. Martha, however, did not graduate. In her junior year she quit. She would later say that her real life began in the spring of 1930, when she boarded a ship bound for Paris. She carried with her a typewriter, a suitcase of clothes, and a little money—seventy-five dollars.

Martha Gellhorn would cross and recross the Atlantic Ocean many times in the years both before and following the Second World War. She never tired of traveling and meeting new people. She never stopped writing. Writing was in her blood. Words flowed through her. When the world was at peace, she wrote about her travels to Africa, Mexico, and Greece. She also wrote novels based on the places she had lived and the people she had met. When the world was at war, she traveled to those violent places and was again a war correspondent. In the Middle East she wrote about refugees in a camp on a stretch of land called the Gaza Strip. In Central America she wrote about government terrorists who arrested and blindfolded citizens, folding them into cars and driving away. She wrote until her death at the age of ninety, in 1999.

A British journalist once described Martha Gellhorn's work this way: "She writes with a cold eye and a warm heart." The cold eye was Martha's focus on vivid details. She didn't soften the blow so that the reader might not be offended. If a child's legs were covered with red sores from poor food and dirty water, then she wrote about it so that the reader could see the sores. The warm heart was her love of people.

She didn't care for politicians. She thought most were "liars." She preferred writing about ordinary people who found themselves the victims of the Great Depression or wars the politicians had started. She did not mock these common people. She did not write about them with pity or scorn. Instead, she wrote about their dignity and their honesty.

After a lifetime of writing about war, she came to understand that most wars are the same. The weapons may differ, the countries and the years may change, but the consequences of war are always the same: hunger, homelessness, fear, and pain.

"There has to be a better way to run the world," she wrote when she was eighty years old. "And we had better see that we get it."

Geyer—known as "Gee Gee"—in 1959, they called her their "new gal on the society desk." Soon, however, she was writing news stories about refugees who fled from a revolution in Hungary, about the new leader of the Soviet Union, Nikita Khrushchev. She traveled to South America to write about the lifestyles of America's southern neighbors. While there, she found herself in the middle of a revolution and so reported on that. In 1966, she interviewed the Communist leader of Cuba, Fidel Castro.

Isabelle Shelton, Denise McCluggage, Gee Gee Geyer, and hundreds of newswomen like them were changing the look and the content of the news. Some newspapers dropped the head "Women's Page" and instead called it "Style" or "Living" or "View."

"Gone are the days of the old-fashioned 'women's pages,'" reported *Time* magazine in 1967. "Taking their place in U.S. newspapers are pages for women filled with news and feature stories about the facts of modern life." Modern life included a long list of social issues of real concern to women: divorce, gambling, alcoholism, child molesters, atomic testing, and new developments in medicine. Men as well as women were reading these feature stories, the *Time* article reported. The women's pages were no longer "fluff." They were newsworthy!

But what of the war correspondents? What was normalcy for them?

Sadly, peace was hard to hold on to. It slipped through the fingers. In the 1950s, a new war erupted in the country of Korea. Marguerite Higgins soon found herself back in military fatigues, reporting from the Korean front lines. Back home, high school student Barbara Belford read the war stories Marguerite Higgins was writing from Korea and thought that being a foreign correspondent must be thrilling. "I dreamed of being another Marguerite Higgins," she said. After graduation from college Barbara knocked on the doors of the *New York Herald Tribune* and got a job.

The women correspondents during the Second World War were all "women with brooms." Whether their assignment was in the newsroom at home or in a field hospital or just behind the front lines overseas, each swept away the stereotypes of what society thought a woman could and could not do. Their brooms were made not of straw and wood but of photographs and words. A broom was a small thing for such a large task, Anne O'Hare McCormick had written of the women in Europe in 1945. And yet the women kept at it.

Even after the war had ended and Americans tried to return to normal lives, the women correspondents kept sweeping, sweeping for change.

> " I have often wondered why I do it, why we do it. After a few seconds, the answer used to come easily: because it's worth it, because it matters, because the world will care once they see our stories. Because if we the storytellers don't do this, then the bad people will win. "
>
> ✶CHRISTIANE AMANPOUR,
> CNN INTERNATIONAL CORRESPONDENT

WAVES OF
CHANGE

History is rarely a straight path from "there" to "here." Instead, history happens in waves that rush forward, then recede. Each wave alters the landscape. The change is not always noticeable at first. In time, however, the transformation can be dramatic.

And so it was with the Second World War. For the first time ever, a wave of women war correspondents rushed forward into the fray. Their words and their photographs battered the old beliefs of what a woman was capable of enduring and understanding during wartime. After the war ended, the wave receded, leaving its mark on the land.

The next wave of war came in 1950. Korea was a poor country of green rice paddies and mountain villages. American troops were part of an international force sent to the Asian country to defend South Korea from the Communists of North Korea. Where soldiers go, so too go the war correspondents.

On an August night in the city of Taejon, an Australian reporter named Jack Percival camped on the floor of a house the military had provided for the press. During the night a fellow correspondent rolled over more than once, crowding Jack's space. Finally, the sleepy reporter gave the other fellow a good shove. That's when he learned that the "fellow" wasn't a fellow at all.

Jack jumped to his feet. Not one but two women correspondents were sleeping on the floor. They were Marguerite Higgins of the *New York Herald Tribune* and Charlotte Knight of *Collier's* magazine. "There are women in here!" Jack shouted.

The reporter's surprise is evidence that women war correspondents were still an unusual occurrence, even five years after the end of the Second World War. Prejudices in that war surfaced again in this new conflict. General Walton H. Walker was the commander of the American forces in South Korea. Just a few weeks earlier he had ordered Marguerite Higgins out of the country. The military did not have time to worry about where a woman might eat and sleep separate from a man, he stated. His reasoning was no different from what Colonel Dupuy had told Dickey Chapelle almost ten years earlier when she had applied for her accreditation as a war photographer. The argument against women war correspondents was still all about latrines, or so it seemed.

When Marguerite protested, the general's staff ordered three armed MPs to escort her to an airplane departing for Toyko. Marguerite's expulsion from Korea triggered negative publicity. Her editors at the *Herald Tribune* were equally sore that their award-winning journalist who had been the first to enter the concentration camp at Dachau was ousted from the war zone. Marguerite met with General MacArthur himself to argue her case. Soon after, the general sent a telegram to the *Herald Tribune*, stating simply: BAN ON WOMEN CORRESPONDENTS IN KOREA HAS BEEN LIFTED. MARGUERITE HIGGINS

IS HELD IN HIGHEST PROFESSIONAL ESTEEM BY EVERYONE.

That's how both Marguerite and Charlotte Knight came to be in the press house that night in Taejon. Like her male counterparts, Marguerite would report from the

Christiane Amanpour is a television news broadcaster who has covered wars in many countries. In this photograph, taken in Israel in 2000, she wears a bullet-proof vest while waiting to make her news broadcast that will air on CNN.

front lines, coming under enemy fire more than once in her effort to witness the war for her readers back home. For one of these stories, she would win journalism's highest honor, the Pulitzer Prize.

The ban on women war correspondents in Korea might have been lifted, but discrimination against women war correspondents would continue for decades more. It would take additional waves, additional women fighting against prejudice, to truly alter the landscape for women journalists. Not until the 1990s during wars in Africa and the Middle East would women come close to standing on equal footing with male correspondents.

One of those women was Molly Moore. In 1991, the *Washington Post* sent Molly to Saudi Arabia to report on the Persian Gulf War. She accompanied American marines as they rolled through Kuwait into Iraq. Although she had written about war, she had never before gone to war. Weeks later, wearing a helmet, flak jacket, and metal dog tags around her neck, she was on the front lines. No one questioned why a woman was there to report the story.

Perhaps the most famous war correspondent today is Christiane Amanpour. For more than twenty years she has reported for the television news agency CNN from war zones in Europe, the Middle East, Africa, and the Carribbean. She has had more active war experience in numbers of assignments and years than most military units. Because CNN broadcasts in most every country in the world, people throughout the world know her. "Wherever I go, people say jokingly, or maybe not so jokingly, that they shudder when they see me," she said. "U.S. soldiers," she added, "joke that they track my movements in order to know where they will be deployed next."

The world sees Christiane Amanpour not as a woman journalist but rather as a war correspondent. Martha Gellhorn would have approved. Interestingly, Martha Gellhorn is one of the war correspondents that Christiane greatly admires.

America's female correspondents during the Second World War were a remarkable group of women. Although they achieved much and shattered many societal stereotypes, they did not single-handedly change the world of journalism for women. Their achievements came as the result of those made by the front-page girls and sob sisters of the 1920s and 1930s. Those early female journalists had opened a door through which the war correspondents entered the scene. In turn, the war correspondents opened the door for those women who followed them in the decades that followed. With each subsequent wave—in Korea and Vietnam, in Somalia and Afghanistan, in Iraq—the door has opened wider still.

FOR FURTHER READING

Here are some interesting websites to browse
for further information and images:

"Dorothea Lange." Feature Exhibit.
Oakland Museum of California.
**www.museumca.org/global/
resources.html.**

Franklin D. Roosevelt Presidential
Library and Museum.
www.fdrlibrary.marist.edu.

Lee Miller Archives.
www.leemiller.co.uk/gallery.aspx.

"The Nizkor Project."
Holocaust Research Guide.
www.nizkor.org.

"Voices of World War II: Experiences
from the Front and at Home."
Original radio broadcasts
presented by the University of
Missouri-Kansas City Libraries.
www.umkc.edu/lib.

"War Stories." Online exhibit
of the Newseum.
**www.newseum.org/warstories/
index.htm.**

"Women Come to the Front." Online
exhibit of the Library of Congress.
www.loc.gov/exhibits/wcf/.

"Women in Journalism." Oral
history project of the Washington
Press Club Foundation.
npc.press.org/wpforal/ohhome.htm.

"World War II Photos." Exhibit of
the National Archives and Records
Administration.
www.archives.gov

PHOTO CREDITS

Allan Richardson, New York, courtesy of Old Dominion University: pp. viii (*bottom row, center*) and 49

The Bancroft Library University of California, Berkeley: pp. viii (*middle row, center*), 55, 59, 63, 65, 66, and 172

Corbis: pp. 128 and 174–75

Corbis/Bettman: pp. 303–301

FDR Library: pp. vi (*second from left*), 8–9, 12

John F. Kennedy Presidential Library and Museum: pp. viii (*bottom row, right*), 14, 162, and 164

Library of Congress, Prints and Photographs Division, FSA/OWI collection: pp. viii (*top row, right*) and 16 (LC-USZ62-128944), pp. 6 and 21 (LC-USF34-9058-C), p. 19 (LC-USZ62-58355), pp. 24 and 28 (LC-USW3-009038-E), pp. vi (*third from left*) and 95 (LC-USZ62-17124)

Library of Congress, Prints and Photographs Division, *New York World-Telegram* and the *Sun* Newspaper Photograph Collection: pp. viii (*top row, center*) and 108 (LC-USZ62-126657); pp. viii (*top row, left*), 102, and 113 (LC-USZ62-126508)

National Archives: pp. 43 (ARC 540153), p. 52 (ARC 559369), p.83 (ARC 520590), p. 89 and 74 (ARC 535800), p. 96 (ARC 536001), p. 77 (ARC 541922), p. 106 (ARC 531351), p. 104 (ARC 531335), pp. 116–17 and 122 (ARC 195515), pp. 142 and 155 (ARC 535795), and p. 157 (ARC 520932)

National Archives/Still Pictures Branch:

pp. 79 (NWDNS-44-PA-2314) and 91 (NWDNS-44-PA-2272)

Office of War Information, courtesy of National Archives: p. 32 (ARC 513828)

Time-Life Pictures/Getty Images: pp. 69, 87, 126, and 166

United States Holocaust Memorial Museum, courtesy of Francis Robert Artz: p. 139

United States Holocaust Memorial Museum, courtesy of Instytut Pamiece Narodowej: p. 57

United States Holocaust Memorial Museum, courtesy of Julia Pirotee: pp. viii (*middle row, left*) and 61

United States Holocaust Memorial Museum, courtesy of the National Archives: pp. vii (*second from right*), 32–33, and 135

United States Holocaust Memorial Museum, courtesy of Richard Freimark: p. 37

United States Holocaust Memorial Museum, courtesy of Rosenbloom: p. 137

U.S. Information Agency, courtesy of National Archives: p. 110 (ARC 541920)

War Relocation Authority, courtesy of National Archives: pp. 98–99 (ARC 539961)

Wisconsin Historical Society: pp. vi (*first from left*), vii (*last on right*), viii (*middle row, right, bottom row, left*), xii, 146, 147, 148–149

NOTES

INTRODUCTION

1. Chapelle, *What's a Woman Doing Here?* pp. 52–53.
2. Cairs, p. 2.
3. Ibid., p. 126.

CHAPTER ONE

1. Gellhorn, "Report from Gaston County, November 11, 1934."
2. Ibid.
3. Meltzer, *Dorothea Lange*, p. 69.
4. Doud, "Interview with Dorothea Lange."
5. Ibid.
6. Lange, *Popular Photography*, February 1960.
7. Quoted in Watkins, *The Hungry Years*, p. 67.
8. Quoted in Meltzer, *Brother, Can You Spare a Dime?* p. 37.

CHAPTER TWO

1. In Ross, *Ladies of the Press*, p. xi.
2. Ibid., p. xii.
3. "White House Journalists."
4. Ibid.
5. Ross, *Ladies of the Press*, pp. 310–311.
6. "The Eleanor Roosevelt Press Conferences."
7. Ibid.
8. "Eleanor Everywhere."
9. Quoted in Kurth, *American Cassandra*, p. 162.
10. Belford, *Brilliant Bylines*, p. 208.
11. Kurth, *American Cassandra*, pp. 199–201.
12. Beck, *No One Lives for Himself.*

13. Thompson, "Something Is Rotten."
14. Thompson, *Dorothy Thompson's Political Guide*, p. 11.
15. "Cartwheel Girl."
16. Quoted in Sheehan, *The World at Home*, p. x.
17. Ibid., p. 279.
18. Quoted in Sheehan, *The Spiritual Woman*, pp. xiii–xiv.
19. Quoted in Cook, *Eleanor Roosevelt*, p. 103.
20. Van Derman, "11 O'Clock, The White House."

CHAPTER THREE

1. Cowles, in *Reporting World War II*, pt. 1, pp. 53–54.
2. Tomara, in *Reporting World War II*, pt. 1, pp. 70–71.
3. Quoted in Fisher, "Therese Bonney Went to War."
4. Quoted in "Therese Bonney," *Current Biography.*
5. Weitz, *Sisters in the Resistance*, p. 1.
6. Ibid., p. 3.
7. Long, "The Free Press of Enslaved Europe," p. 20.
8. Ibid., pp. 20, 21, 38.
9. Nizkor Project, "Murder and Ill-Treatment."
10. Ibid., quoting a statement made by Himmler in 1943.
11. Bonney, *Europe's Children.*
12. Rubin, *Margaret Bourke-White*, p. 66.
13. Bourke-White, *Portrait of Myself,* pp. 175–176.

14. Ibid., p. 177.

15. Bourke-White, in *Reporting World War II*, pt. 1, p. 198.

16. Ibid., pp. 200–202.

CHAPTER FOUR

1. From Helen Kirkpatrick's oral history interview with the Washington Press Club Foundation.

2. Ibid.

3. Kirkpatrick, "Battle in Famed Paris Cathedral Told: On-Spot," *Chicago Daily News*, September 9, 1940.

4. Gellhorn, *The Face of War*, p. 79.

5. "Voices of World War II."

6. Ibid.

7. Norman, *We Band of Angels*, p. 5.

8. Shelley Mydans, "Defenders of Philippines," p. 30.

9. "A Letter from the Publisher," *Time*, December 28, 1942.

10. Frank and Sann, "Paper Dolls," p. 20.

11. Quoted in Frank and Sann, "Paper Dolls," p. 93.

12. Higgins, *News Is a Singular Thing*, pp. 18–25.

13. Ibid., p. 56.

14. Quoted in Handley and Lewis, *True West*, p. 241.

15. Quoted by the Constitutional Rights Foundation, in "Wartime and the Bill of Rights: The Korematsu Case," www.crf-usa.org/terror/korematsu.htm.

16. Quoted in *San Francisco Chronicle*, May 21, 1942, as posted online at Virtual Museum of the City of San Francisco, www.sfmuseum.org/war/evactxt.html.

17. Quoted in Meltzer, *Dorothea Lange*, p. 243.

18. Quoted in "Dorothea Lange," Oakland Museum of California, www.museumca.org/global/art/collections_dorothea_lange.html.

CHAPTER FIVE

1. Frissell, *Toni Frissell*, p. xxvi.

2. Ibid.

3. Ibid., p. 31.

4. Reprinted in *Reporting World War II*, pt. 2, p. 721

5. Gellhorn, "Children Are Soldiers, Too," *Collier's*, sec. 113:21+, March 4, 1944.

6. Gellhorn, "Three Poles," in *The Face of War*, p. 97.

7. Ibid., p. 99.

8. Ibid., p. 100.

9. Ibid., p. 101.

10. Kirkpatrick, oral history interview, Washington Press Club Foundation.

11. Reprinted in *Reporting World War II*, pt. 2, p. 151; originally published as Martha Gellhorn, "The First Hospital Ship," *Collier's*, August 5, 1944.

12. "Voices of World War II."

13. Ibid.

14. Moorehead, *Gellhorn*, p. 219.

15. Gellhorn, *The Face of War*, p. 86.

CHAPTER SIX

1. Litoff and Smith, *We're in This War, Too*, p. 159.

2. Penrose, *Lee Miller's War*, p. 16.

3. Ibid., pp. 20–23.

4. Ibid., p. 24.

5. Ibid., p. 92.

6. Ibid., p. 39.

7. Ibid., p. 36.

8. Ibid., p. 48.

9. Kirkpatrick, oral history interview, Washington Press Club Foundation.

10. Flanner, "Letter from Paris."

11. Ibid.

12. Reprinted in *Reporting World War II*, pt. 2, p. 603; originally published as Martha Gellhorn, *The Face of War*, p. 145.

13. Ibid., p. 606.

14. Penrose, *Lee Miller's War*, pp. 92–93

15. Ibid., p. 161.

16. Reprinted in *Reporting World War II*, pt. 2, pp. 681–682; originally aired as Edward Murrow, "For Most of It I Have No Words," CBS Radio broadcast, April 15, 1945.

17. Higgins, *News Is a Singular Thing*, pp. 89–90.

18. "33,000 Dachau Captives Freed by 7th Army," *New York Herald Tribune*, May 1, 1945.

19. Reprinted in *Reporting World War II*, pt. 2, p. 724; originally published as Martha Gellhorn, "Dachau," *Collier's*, June 23, 1945.

20. Moorehead, *Gellhorn*, p. 240.

21. Ibid.

CHAPTER SEVEN

1. Quoted in Toland, *Adolf Hitler*, p. 870.

2. Chapelle, *What's a Woman Doing Here?*, p. 49.

3. Ibid., pp. 77–79.

4. In Ostroff, *Fire in the Wind*, p. 99.

5. Ibid., p. 80.

6. "A Letter from the Publisher," *Time*, December 31, 1945.

7. Harry S. Truman Library, "Army Press Notes."

8. Ibid.

9. Ibid.

10. "Story Over."

CHAPTER EIGHT

1. McCormick, "Bulldozer and the Women with the Broom."

2. "A Letter from the Publisher," *Time*, July 2, 1945.

3. Moorehead, *Gellhorn*, p. 253.

SELECT BIBLIOGRAPHY

Beck, Heinz R. *No One Lives for Himself: Memories, 1925–1945.* World War II Lecture Institute. www.wwiilectureinstitute.com/stories/beck.htm.

Belford, Barbara. *Brilliant Bylines: A Biographical Anthology of Notable Newspaperwomen in America.* New York: Columbia University Press, 1986.

Bernstein, Mark, and Alex Lubertozzi. *World War II on the Air: Edward Murrow and the Broadcasts That Riveted a Nation.* Naperville, IL: Sourcebooks, Inc., 2003.

Bonney, Therese M. *Europe's Children.* New York: Plantin Press, Co., 1943.

Bourke-White, Margaret. "Death and Life on the Battlefields." *Reporting World War II.* Part 1: *American Journalism, 1938–1944.* New York: Library of America, 1995, pp. 106–210.

———. *Portrait of Myself.* New York: Simon & Schuster, Inc., 1963.

Cairns, Kathleen A. *Front-Page Women Journalists, 1920–1950.* Lincoln: University of Nebraska Press, 2003.

"Cartwheel Girl." *Time*, vol. xxxiii, no. 24, June 12, 1939.

Chapelle, Dickey. *What's a Woman Doing Here?* New York: William Morrow & Co., 1962.

"Christiane Amanpour Addresses RTNDA 2000 Attendees." Radio-Television News Directors Association & Foundation, September 28, 2000. www.rtnda.org.

Cook, Blanche Wiese. *Eleanor Roosevelt.* Vol. 2: *1933–1938.* New York: Viking, 1999.

Curtis, James. *Mind's Eye, Mind's Truth: FSA Photography Reconsidered.* Philadelphia: Temple University Press, 1989.

"Denise McCluggage: Welcome to the Automotive Hall of Fame!" *Road & Travel Magazine*, 2004. www.roadandtravel.com/celebrities/denisemccluggage_autohall.htm.

Doud, Richard K. "Interview with Dorothea Lange." Conducted for the Smithsonian Institution, May 22, 1964. archivesofamericanart.si.edu.

Downes, Bruce. "Europe's Children: Therese Bonney

Photographs Nazi Victims, and Makes a Dramatic Book of Photographs." *Popular Photography,* vol. 7, December 1943.

"Eleanor Everywhere." *Time,* November 20, 1933.

"The Eleanor Roosevelt Press Conferences." Oral history collection, featuring interviews with Ann Cottrell Free, Frances Lide, Ruth Montgomery, and Malvina Stephenson. Washington Press Club Foundation, May 22, 1989.

Finney, Ruth. "Doors Open for Women." *Independent Woman* 22 (January 1943): 5–6.

Fisher, Barbara E. Scott. "Therese Bonney Went to War with a Camera and Came Back with Fame." *Christian Science Monitor,* February 18, 1941.

Flanner, Janet. "Letter from Paris." *New Yorker,* December 23, 1944, pp. 42–47.

Frank, Stanley, and Paul Sann. "Paper Dolls." *Saturday Evening Post,* May 23, 1944, pp. 20+.

Frissell, Toni. *Toni Frissell:* Photographs, 1933–1967. New York: Doubleday, 1967.

Gellhorn, Martha. "Children Are Soldiers, Too." *Collier's,* March 4, 1944, pp. 21+.

____. *The Face of War.* New York: Atlantic Monthly Press, 1988.

____. "Over and Back." *Collier's,* July 22, 1944, p. 16.

____. "Report from Gaston County, North Carolina, November 11, 1934." Franklin D. Roosevelt Library, Hopkins Papers, Box 66.

____. "Report from Gaston County, North Carolina, November 19, 1934."

Franklin D. Roosevelt Library, Hopkins Papers, Box 66. Gordon, Herbert. "Women Are Writing the News!" *Christian Science Monitor,* September 25, 1943, p. 5.

Handley, William R., and Nathaniel Lewis, eds. *True West: Authenticity and the American West.* Lincoln: University of Nebraska Press, 2004.

Harry S. Truman Library. "Army Press Notes." Box 4, papers of Eben A. Ayers. Posted online as "White House Press Release Announcing the Bombing of Hiroshima, August 6, 1945: Statement by the President of the United States," www.pbs.org/wgbh/amex/truman/psources/ps_pressrelease.html.

"Helen Keller Warns Germany's Students; Says Burning of Books Cannot Kill Ideas." *New York Times*, May 10, 1933, p. 10.

Higgins, Marguerite. "33,000 Dachau Captives Freed by 7th Army." *New York Herald Tribune*, May 1, 1945. © by The New York Times Co. Excerpts reprinted with permission.

___. *News Is a Singular Thing.* New York: Doubleday, 1955.

"Janet Flanner." *Current Biography: Who's News and Why*, 1943, pp. 204-206.

Kennedy, David. *Freedom from Fear: The American People in Depression and War, 1929–1945.* New York: Oxford University Press, 1999.

Kirkpatrick, Helen. "Battle in Famed Paris Cathedral Told: On-Spot Story." *Chicago Daily News*, September 9, 1940.

___. "Daily News Writer Sees Man Slain at Her Side in Hail of Lead." *Chicago Daily News*, August 26, 1944.

___. Oral history interview. Washington Press Club Foundation, April 3, 1990.

Kurth, Peter. *American Cassandra: The Life of Dorothy Thompson.* Boston: Little, Brown & Co., 1990.

Lange, Dorothea. "The Assignment I'll Never Forget." *Popular Photography*, 1960, pp. 42-43+.

Lash, Joseph P. *A World of Love: Eleanor Roosevelt and Her Friends, 1943–62.* New York: Doubleday, 1984.

Litoff, Judy Barrett, and David C. Smith. *We're in This War, Too: World War II Letters from American Women in Uniform.* New York: Oxford University Press, 1994.

Long, Tania. "The Free Press of Enslaved Europe." *New York Times* magazine, May 16, 1943, pp. 20-1+.

Marzolf, Marion. *Up from the Footnote: A History of Women Journalists.* New York: Communication Arts Books, Hastings House, 1977.

May, Antoinette. *Witness to War: A Biography of Marguerite Higgins, the Legendary Pulitzer Prize–Winning War Correspondent.* New York: Penguin Books, 1983.

McCormick, Anne O'Hare. "Bulldozer and the Women with the Broom." *New York Times*, March 28, 1945.

Meltzer, Milton. *Brother, Can You Spare a Dime?* New York: Alfred A. Knopf, 1969.

___. *Dorothea Lange: A Photographer's Life.* New York: Farrar, Straus, and Giroux, 1978.

Moorehead, Caroline. *Gellhorn: A Twentieth-Century Life.* New York: Henry Holt, 2003.

Mydans, Carl. *Carl Mydans, Photojournalist.* New York: Harry N. Abrams, 1985.

Mydans, Shelley. "Defenders of Philippines." *Life*, December 22, 1941.

Nizkor Project. "Murder and Ill-Treatment of Civilian Population." www.Nizkor.org.

Norman, Elizabeth. *We Band of Angels: The Untold Story of American Nurses Trapped on Bataan by the Japanese.* New York: Random House, 1999.

Ostroff, Roberta. *Fire in the Wind: The Life of Dickey Chapelle.* Annapolis, MD: Bluejacket Books, 1992.

Penrose, Anthony, ed. *Lee Miller's War: Photographer and Correspondent with the Allies in Europe, 1944–45.* Boston: Bulfinch/Little Brown, 1992.

Text and photographs © by Lee Miller Archives, England, 2005. Reprinted by kind permission of Thames & Hudson Ltd., London, and Palazzo Editions Ltd., Bath.

Riess, Curt, ed. *They Were There: The Story of World War II and How It Came About, by America's Foremost Correspondents.* New York: Books for Libraries Press, 1944.

Reporting World War II. Part 1: *American Journalism, 1938–1944* and part 2: *American Journalism, 1944–1946.* New York: Library of America, 1995.

Rogers St. Johns, Adela. *Some Are Born Great.* New York: Doubleday, 1974.

Roosevelt, Eleanor. "Keepers of Democracy." *Virginia Quarterly Review* 15 (January 1939): 105.

Ross, Ishbel. *Ladies of the Press.* New York: Harper & Bros., 1936.

Rubin, Susan Goldman. *Margaret Bourke-White.* New York: Henry N. Abrams, 1999.

"Ruby Black." The Handbook of Texas Online. www.tsha.utexas.edu.

Schlipp, Madelon Golden, and Sharon M. Murphy. *Great Women of the Press*. Carbondale: Southern Illinois University Press, 1983.

Sheehan, Marion Turner. *The Spiritual Woman: Trustee of the Future*. New York: Harper, 1955.

___. ed. *The World at Home: Selections from the Writings of Anne O'Hare McCormick*. Freeport, NY: Books for Libraries Press, 1956.

Shelton, Isabelle. Oral history interview. Washington Press Club Foundation, July 30, 1992, September 2, 1992, and November 11, 1992.

Simms, William Philip. "Starvation Weapon." *New York Times*, Book Review Section, March 26, 1944.

"Skirted: Exclusion of Women from White House Correspondents' Dinner." *Time*, March 13, 1944, p. 83.

Stone, Matt. "A Race Named Denise." *Road & Travel Magazine*, 2004. www.roadandtravel.com/celebrities/denise_mccluggage.html. "Story Over." *Time*, April 30, 1945.

Sorel, Nancy Caldwell. *The Women Who Wrote the War*. New York: Arcade Publishing, 1999.

"Therese Bonney." *Current Biography: Who's News and Why*, 1944, pp. 51–54.

Thompson, Dorothy. *Dorothy Thompson's Political Guide: A Study of American Liberalism and Its Relationship to Modern Totalitarian States*. New York: Stackpole Sons, 1938.

___. *Let the Record Speak*. Boston: Houghton Mifflin, 1939.

Toland, John. *Adolf Hitler*. New York: Doubleday, 1976.

"Tomboy with a Typewriter." *Time*, April 8, 1957.

Van Derman, Ruth. "11 O'Clock, The White House." *Smith Alumnae Quarterly* 27 (November 1935). Reprinted in *SAQ Online*; saqonline.smith.edu/.

"Voices of World War II: Experiences from the Front and at Home." Original radio broadcasts presented by the University of Missouri-Kansas City Libraries, Miller Nichols Library, Marr Sound Archives, Department of Special Collections. www.umkc.edu/lib/spec-col/ww2/index.htm. Excerpts reprinted with permission of the University of Missouri-Kansas City Libraries.

Watkins, T. H. *The Hungry Years.*
New York: Henry Holt, 1999.

Weitz, Margaret Collins. *Sisters
in the Resistance: How Women
Fought to Free France, 1940–
1945.* New York: John Wiley & Sons,
Inc., 1995.

"White House Journalists,"
featuring Ruby Black. Library
of Congress, in Literature and
Journalism Collection, Manuscript
Division. memory.loc.gov/ammem/
awhhtml/awmss5/wh_journ.html.

Witherspoon, Frances. "Horror of
Horrors." *New York Times*, Book
Review Section, March 26, 1944.

INDEX